Stadium Stories:
Washington State Cougars

Stadium Stories™ Series

Stadium Stories:
Washington State Cougars

Bud Withers

INSIDERS' GUIDE®

GUILFORD, CONNECTICUT
AN IMPRINT OF THE GLOBE PEQUOT PRESS

INSIDERS' GUIDE®

Text design: Casey Shain
All photos are courtesy of WSU Athletics.
Cover photos: *front cover:* Drew Bledsoe; *back cover:* top, coach Babe Hollingbery and Glenn "Turk" Edwards; bottom, Jason Gesser.

Library of Congress Cataloging-in-Publication Data

Withers, Bud.
    Stadium stories : Washington State Cougars / Bud Withers. — 1st ed.
    p. cm. — (Stadium stories series)
    ISBN-13: 978-0-7627-3975-2
    ISBN-10: 0-7627-3975-4
    1. Washington State University—Football—History. 2. Washington State Cougars (Football team)—History. I. Title. II. Series.

GV958.W38W57 2006
796.332'630979739—dc22   2006041830

Manufactured in the United States of America
First Edition/First Printing

Contents

This book is for all those who manage to
get a lot out of a little.

Introduction

Legend has it that when the Washington State football job opened up in 1956 after a series of fallow seasons, one of those who threw his hat into the ring—a top hat, probably—was William "Lone Star" Dietz. He was the Carlisle Indian who built a 17–2–1 record and coached the Cougars to their only Rose Bowl victory, in 1917.

As job applicants go, the dapper Dietz was along in years—72, in fact. Who knows what he might have been thinking? He had left WSU almost four decades earlier under unusual circumstances; shortly after World War I, a Spokane jury acquitted him of charges he had misrepresented his Indian heritage and evaded the draft.

Dietz became a silversmith, a teacher, a theater critic, a motivational speaker. Lord knows why he might have been moved to try to recapture something from his past. He didn't get the job, and his mindset will remain a delicious mystery.

Say this about Dietz's septuagenarian pursuit of the position won by Jim Sutherland: It might take a Cougar to understand. For decades now, WSU grads have been coming back, tangibly and in spirit, to a place with a hold on them.

"I loved the school," says Jim Sweeney, the colorful former football coach, "and I still do." This is a man who once won two games in two seasons, whose team allowed 232 points in a four-game stretch. No matter. Sweeney found reward in the quest, ultimately winning as many as seven games and validating the wacko enthusiasm with which he tackled the job.

Taking over after the 1967 season, Sweeney used to bring the weekend's football recruits to basketball games at Bohler Gym, a roiling gathering place during the best years of coach Marv Harshman. Madly, Sweeney would strip off his sports jacket and lead the crowd in a spell-out of "Cougars." Right after that, he would grab a microphone and drag the fans through a song that began, "I've got that Cougar spirit, deep in my heart. . . ." No, it wasn't written by Paul Simon. But somehow, it made consecutive losses in 1970, 54–9 to UCLA and 70–33 to USC, slide down a little more easily.

Jim Owens, the icon coach at Washington, used to tell Sweeney that he'd eventually run out of gas. Sure enough, Sweeney did in 1975, but not before he'd taken Owens down with him, one year pitching a virtual shutout of the state's best recruits. "It can wear you down," Sweeney conceded, referring to the particular demands of being a WSU head football coach. "I had opportunities to leave. I never regretted it. I loved the school."

Make no mistake, WSU isn't for everybody. Pullman is the butt of an old one-liner, perhaps first uttered by the late Dr. Leo Bustad, dean of the WSU School of Veterinary Medicine: "It's not the end of the earth. But you can see it from there."

Shawn McWashington, a Seattle product and one of the "Fab Five" receivers of the 1997 Rose Bowl team, struggled for a long time with everything from football to an unfamiliarity with the food. He considered leaving. Eventually, what won him over was the people; he even grew to know the president, Sam Smith, whose door he found open to conversation.

Rueben Mayes, the record-setting running back, took a job in external relations for the University of Washington's business school. After a brief stint there, he and his wife Marie returned to Pullman, where he is in development in the office of undergraduate education. "We have a mission statement," Mayes says. "We decided to move to Pullman, because that's where we want to raise our family. [Marie] hated moving at first. Now I couldn't pry her away."

Jack Thompson, the consummate Cougar, believes there's a kind of silent symbiosis between the farmers of Whitman County and the students at WSU, resulting in the development of a work ethic. "I believe our school is a breeding ground for good people with great values," says Thompson. "We're all there under the same circumstances; it forces us to get to know each other. We're all away from home but close enough to home that your parents can come there at any minute and crack you over the head. That's how I felt."

Maybe, too, that's how his son Tony feels. The younger Thompson, a walk-on tight end, was asked by his father in 2005 whether he was fitting in, whether he missed home. Tony Thompson demurred. "You raised me," he said. "This is where I belong."

Part of Jack Thompson's recruitment to WSU had nothing to do with football or whether he could start as a freshman. He was chatting with his family doctor about college choices.

"Where are you going to live the rest of your life?" the doctor asked.

"Seattle—you know that," Thompson replied.

"Well, then you need to go to Washington State University," the doctor said. "You need to go absorb a different lifestyle. You're going to be citified for the rest of your life. You need to breathe that air."

It wasn't so much the air but the coziness that won over Jason David, the cornerback who helped the Cougars win thirty games from 2001 to 2003. "What I thought was neat about Pullman was, there were so many students there," he said after his rookie season with the Indianapolis Colts. "You go to the grocery store, and you may see somebody from your English class. You go to the gas station, and there's somebody from your psychology class. People recognized you. It was a lot of fun."

The truth is that a lot of WSU's football history includes far less compelling seasons than those David knew. The Cougars, by turns, have been very good, sometimes very bad, and often, somewhere in between. Winning there is certifiably difficult; the Cougars didn't have a post-season drought of fifty-one years (1930–1981) for nothing.

On the other hand, as the most isolated Division 1-A program competing in a league with urban schools, you'd have to conclude WSU has overperformed. The Cougars haven't fired a football coach since 1967, far longer ago than any other school in the Pac-10. In the 1970s, there was a groundswell of opinion that it was a losing proposition for the Pac-10 to subsidize Washington State, Oregon State, and Oregon. While OSU was only beginning a dreary, twenty-eight-year skein of losing seasons, and Oregon didn't really know its renaissance until the late 1980s, it was WSU that went to a bowl game in 1981, had the best team in the league (7–4) at the end of 1983—even if it didn't go anywhere—and won nine games in 1988.

Moreover, hardly anybody seems to have as much fun going about it as the Cougars. Seemingly, it's been a place where the head coach—from Jim Sweeney to Jim Walden to Mike Price—has had a sense of humor, a knack for the sound bite, and a facility for a quote well delivered.

Perhaps because the destination isn't always gilded, the

Cougars appreciate the journey more than most. To those who have known the wonders of Pullman, maybe that's one of the things that brings them back. Bill Doba's first staff at WSU included five alumni.

"If the right circumstance happened," said Ron Lee, a safety in the late 1980s and now an assistant coach at Wisconsin, "I wouldn't be afraid to go back to Pullman."

Guess what? Neither would Jason Gesser, the career passing leader. "My ultimate goal is to be a quarterback coach there," he said. "An OC [offensive coordinator], maybe even a head coach."

It's a yearning Lone Star Dietz would appreciate.

Leather Helmets, Legendary Figures

Washington State football sidelines have been peopled by some characters, from Jim Sweeney to Jim Walden. Probably the first of the genre was William H. "Lone Star" Dietz—coach, artist, actor, and the most prominent icon of the early days of WSU football.

Not that he was first. In fact, WSU lists him as only the four-teenth coach in school history, following a formative period when "coaches" often played the game themselves. Washington State accords the honor of first coach in 1894 to William Goodyear, publisher of the *Palouse City News*, a weekly newspa-per in the nearby town of Palouse.

Coaches came and went freely in those days. WSU's first of note was John Bender, whose 1906 team was unbeaten (6–0), untied, and unscored upon. Bender left after the 1907 season, returning for a three-year stint in 1912. Burdened by too many duties—including supervising the student newspaper and the yearbook—he was cut loose without a winning season.

Enter Dietz, grandly. "In the summer of 1915, a strikingly handsome, well-built man with the bearing and movements of a well-conditioned athlete stepped down from a passenger train arriving at the Northern Pacific depot in Pullman, Washington," Dick Fry writes in his history of WSU athletics, *The Crimson and the Gray*. "He was wearing a smartly tailored three-piece suit and a pearl grey homburg." He also had so much baggage, trunks, and cases laden with clothes that there wasn't room for all of it at the boarding house on College Hill.

If there weren't so much legend and lore surrounding Dietz, he might simply have been known as one of the best football coaches of his time. His first WSU team went 7–0, allowed 10 points, and won the only Rose Bowl victory in the school's his-tory, 14–0 over Brown.

Dietz, an exponent of the fabled Pop Warner, had installed Warner's single-wing offense to great results. Among the leaders were tackle Ace Clark of Pullman, a future state legislator, and end Clarence Zimmerman of Everett. Carl "Red" Dietz of Bremerton (no relation to the coach), who played halfback, fullback, and end, was voted most valuable and most inspirational by his teammates.

Dietz's impact was so resounding that two of his successors would be products of the Carlisle Indian School in Pennsylvania as the Cougars tried to duplicate the formula he developed in a three-year stint that yielded a 17–2–1 record.

Dietz was born in 1884 to a German civil engineer and a mother who was half Oglala Sioux Indian. The son would play high school football in Wisconsin and Minnesota and later with the legendary Jim Thorpe at Carlisle. He assisted Pop Warner at Carlisle from 1912 to 1914.

Not only was Dietz a clothes horse, he had an eye for the day's paparazzi, such as they were. He would don full Indian garb, including headdress, for the cameras. Or they might catch him in formal attire, with top hat.

Dietz's 1917 team might have been even better (they went 6–0–1 and allowed a single field goal), but the demands

A product of the Carlisle Indian School, William Dietz was usually more than happy to oblige photographers.

of World War I prevented it from a repeat trip to the Rose Bowl. A year later Dietz, coaching the Mare Island Marines, had another team in Pasadena, losing 17–0.

About that time, he suffered a greater defeat. According to research by Pennsylvanian Tom Benjey, author of a book on Dietz, the coach was in a Spokane diner when he was criticized by another man named J. C. Argell for using too much sugar, a

The 1915 Cougars, flanking coach William Dietz (with cane), went unbeaten and shut out Brown in the Rose Bowl.

rationed commodity. An argument ensued. Later, according to Benjey, Argell was appointed head of the local draft board, and citing a newspaper story in the *Portland Oregonian* that questioned whether Dietz was really Indian, Argell took issue with Dietz's registration as a "non-citizen Indian."

He was indicted but, according to Fry, acquitted by a 9–3 vote. By then, though, WSU had withdrawn support for the coach. "It was just one of those prejudice-laden affairs," Fry told the *Seattle Times* in 2005.

That year, after a push by Benjey and the founders of the WSU fan Web site cougfan.com, Dietz was put on the ballot for the College Football Hall of Fame, but he fell short. Surely the passage of long decades have hurt Dietz's chances, although he may remain on the ballot. Septuagenarian John Ralston, the former Stanford coach and a member of the selection committee, said, "He's certainly qualified to be in the Hall of Fame."

■ ■ ■

Who is the greatest coach in Washington State history? Dietz deserves consideration, and for taking the Cougars to two Rose Bowl appearances in six seasons, so does Mike Price. Many historians, however, would opt for Orin E. "Babe" Hollingbery, the longest-tenured (1926–42) of all WSU football coaches. He took the team to the 1931 Rose Bowl, which for decades and through several near misses, became the Holy Grail of WSU teams. For sheer stature and force of personality, he is probably unparalleled.

Paying tribute to Hollingbery when his adopted hometown of Yakima, Washington, honored him with a "day" in 1962, legendary basketball coach Jack Friel wrote, "I well remember the early 1920s when WSC football was at a low ebb. The spirits of the student body and fans were depressed and there was a real need for a new deal. When you came to Pullman in 1926, you brought just what the doctor ordered in the way of coaching ability, aggressive leadership, and cooperation. Soon everybody knew that Cougar teams would be well prepared and ready to give any team a real contest. Your confidence permeated your squads year after year and WSC became a real power in Coast football."

What launched Hollingbery at WSU was perhaps a single victory. But what a victory. He was coach of the Olympic Club, a collection of postcollegians and otherwise unaffiliated players in San Francisco. In 1925, Hollingbery's team took down Andy Smith's storied Cal program, 15–0, handing Smith his first loss since 1919 and dealing the Bears their first defeat in Memorial Stadium.

"Because of that victory, they noticed him at Washington State," said his son Buster, who played for his father in the early 1940s. "They were going to pay him $7,500. He didn't want a contract; it was a handshake. He said, 'If I don't like it and I want to leave, or if you don't like me, you get somebody else.'"

As it turned out, the relationship lasted well beyond that tentative beginning. His son says the Cougars raised his salary to $9,500, and it stayed there throughout his tenure in Pullman, even through at least one romance with another job. "In 1938, the Detroit Lions flew him back to Detroit, interviewed him and offered him the job at $35,000," his son says. When the senior Hollingbery returned, he told his wife he wasn't accepting the offer. "I promised the parents of the boys I was going to look after

Babe Hollingbery was the longest tenured (1926–42) and arguably the best coach in WSU history.

them," Buster Hollingbery quoted his father as saying. "And I can't do it from Detroit."

Babe the Benefactor

If you played for Babe Hollingbery, you belonged to an elite fraternity. There was a designation given to those warriors: You were one of his "boys."

"He talked to parents, convinced the parents to send their kids up here," said his son, Buster Hollingbery. "He found them places to live, jobs for their wives if they were married. And he loaned them one hell of a lot of money."

Hollingbery's era at WSU (1926–42) was one which predated NCAA enforcement. Conference rules nationwide were only loosely enforced. Buster Hollingbery executed many of the last affairs of his father upon his death and said, "I wrote up over $100,000 worth of notes that kids never paid him back. He never asked for it or anything. Some would pay it back and some wouldn't.

"None of it was a gift; he wouldn't do that. They'd sign a note. I had quite a fight with the Internal Revenue Service, but they finally allowed it."

Some of the money was loaned when the players were in school, some after they had left. "He was good that way with kids," the younger Hollingbery says. "He made sure they were taken care of."

It was those sorts of principles by which Hollingbery operated religiously. He forbade smoking, drinking, or swearing during the season. On the training table, there was a pot of coins, fed with nickels, dimes, and quarters, a fund mounting on the severity of the expletive uttered by the players.

"For him," says Rod Giske, a guard and linebacker in the 1940s, "a swear word was, 'Oh, golly.'"

Once, his son was standing at the local post office with Nick Susoeff, a third-team AP All-American in 1941 at end. Susoeff was about to take a drag on a cigarette when he saw the coach's car approaching. "Nick saw the car and just swallowed the cigarette," said Buster Hollingbery. "It didn't matter who you were, a rule was a rule."

At WSU, he ran single wing-based offenses and defenses that featured five-, six-, and sometimes seven-man lines. Generally, he held to the theory that a good defense would always keep you in the game. The "loose seven" defense may have even borne some similarities to today's zone blitz; Buster Hollingbery, a linebacker, remembers hitting the opposing center and then backing straight up.

The younger Hollingbery came to know how hard it could be, a son playing for a father. As a high school player, he took part in spring practice with the Cougars. Then there was the day Buster Hollingbery broke his nose in a punt-blocking drill, catching the punter's foot as well as the ball. "Blood's coming out all over," he said. "I look back, and here's Babe standing there, laughing like hell. I got so damn mad. He thought it was funny."

His son was called for a clip one time at Stanford on a play on which the Cougars gained 50 yards. Buster knew Babe had to be steaming. "He didn't say a word to me on the bench, didn't say anything on the train," his son recalls. "The next day in Portland, we had a team meeting and he didn't say anything. "Then he started in on me, and he never stopped for ten years."

Train schedules, Babe Hollingbery knew. When the Cougars would travel to road games and make forty-five-minute stops, he would always have a football available. Each unit would run plays up and down the platform.

Babe Hollingbery seemed to have a sixth sense about the pulse of his players. He became renowned for rescuing the player from the edge of leaving the team or quitting school. Ron Broom, a sportswriter for the *Evergreen* and later an editor at the *Spokane Chronicle*, related this story on the occasion of Hollingbery's "day" in 1962: "The scene was a fraternity house down Campus Avenue. Study hours had started, and the living room, dimly lighted, was deserted except for two of us. With me was a totally discouraged sophomore backfield candidate. You'd given him a chance to run the first or second outfit in scrimmage that afternoon. He'd looked terrible.

"Disgusted with himself, he said he'd turned in his stuff and was leaving school. He wasn't going to waste anybody's time another day. He wasn't that important, he said. This was a buddy of mine, and of course, I argued with him. He wasn't listening.

"To be truthful, he didn't look very important, as football players go. He was a compact 160 pounds or so. He had some speed and could block. But he did not kick, pass, or carry the ball much; he wasn't tall enough to be ideal on deep defense.

"While we talked, the front bell rang. You were at the door. You walked in, sat down, began talking to him. He was startled.

"You advised him to think it over. You didn't promise him a thing. What you did do was to show this kid he meant something to you. A coach with bigger and better football players and with a lot of other things to do still had time for this. The fellow stayed in school.

"He didn't play a dime's worth that season. He sat, and sat, and sat, every Saturday. He played a little more the next season, but still he sat a good deal. He soaked up knowledge; he got tougher; he prepared for duty."

Summing up the story about Bill Tonkin in 1930, Broom wrote, "Yes, Bill did play all the way in his final season—he quarterbacked the Cougars to the Rose Bowl."

Hollingbery's corollary coaching career to that at WSU was in San Francisco. He was one of the cofounders of the East-West Shrine game benefiting handicapped children. He coached the West team for some two decades and after that was on the selection committee that named the coaches and players. At the 1974 game, in fact, they memorialized the coach with the Hollingbery Medal, given to a player or coach who goes on to distinguish himself. The first winner was President Gerald Ford.

Of course, there was a side benefit to those trips to the Bay Area. Hollingbery used them to recruit prospective talent to Washington State. "He'd talk the language," said Giske. "He'd get 'em in a good mood and the first thing you knew, he had 'em up in Pullman."

"He was very colorful, and the San Francisco area really gave him a lot of press," said Buster Hollingbery. "He was always recruiting. He'd convinced the parents to send their kids up there."

These were some of the finest of Hollingbery's players: Mel Hein (1928–30), the center who is probably the greatest player in school history; tackle Glenn "Turk" Edwards (1929–31); guard Harold Ahlskog (1928–30); quarterback Ed Goddard, who won All-America recognition (1934–36); end Dale Gentry (1938–41); and fullback Bob Kennedy (1940–42).

A member of both the college and pro football halls of fame, Mel Hein is widely considered the best center ever to play the game.

Giske, mindful of how USC would fill an entire sideline in the pregame lineup while WSU had a thirty-man travel squad, mirthfully recalls Kennedy's bravado when the Cougars took an early lead against the vaunted Trojans in 1942. "Let's run it up on 'em," Kennedy exhorted blithely. USC won, 26–12.

It was that sort of USC depth that made so much sweeter one of Hollingbery's—and WSU's—all-time signature victories. On October 11, 1930, the Cougars hosted a Howard Jones–coached USC team that scored 382 points that year. The Trojans beat a 9–1 Stanford team, 41–12, and slaughtered Cal, 74–0. USC went 8–2, losing to WSU and Notre Dame.

Hein, recalling the game with Fry in 1987, says the Cougars played only fourteen men on a warm day in Pullman in front of 22,000. Ahead 7–6 after USC scored its touchdown in the fourth quarter, the Cougars protected the lead when they swarmed the conversion-kick attempt after a bad snap. Finally, WSU end Stub Jones made an open-field tackle of USC quarterback Orville Mohler at the Washington State 12 as the game ended, and the spent Cougars survived.

Besides Hein, Edwards, Ahlskog, and Tonkin, that 1930 team featured captain and second-team All-American Elmer Schwartz at fullback and Carl "Tuffy" Ellingsen at halfback. Those two had originally enrolled at Washington before transferring to WSU. The USC game was the season's defining moment, capped at Washington with a scant 3–0 victory achieved on Lyle Maskell's 43-yard field goal after the Huskies fumbled the opening kickoff.

That earned the Cougars their only undefeated regular season in their last eighty-eight years of playing football. Alas, it evaporated with Alabama's 24–0 victory in the Rose Bowl, when the

Crimson Tide struck for three second-quarter touchdowns using an effective passing game. The Cougars were not themselves, nor was Hollingbery, bundled on the sideline with what historian Rube Samuelsen called a near-pneumonia-like condition.

That was the best of the Hollingbery years. But he didn't suffer a losing season until 1938, and after another one in 1939, it appeared the Cougars were on an uptick by World War II, going 6–4 in 1941 and 6–2–2 in 1942. They finished the 1941 season on December 6 in Tacoma against Texas A&M, losing 7–0. The next day found them riding a train back to Pullman when the news broke.

Babe Hollingbery (left) and Glenn "Turk" Edwards each had his own huge role in WSU's march to the Rose Bowl in 1930.

"We interrupt this program to bring you the President of the United States," came the advisory over the radio. President Franklin Roosevelt relayed the sobering events: Japan had attacked Pearl Harbor, and the United States was at war.

The Cougars played on in 1942, ending with a 21–0 loss at Texas A&M. Buster Hollingbery remembers a near-strike by some of the seniors, who were upset that the team was pulling out of San Antonio by train that night rather than staying over.

His father left the team in Denver to attend conference meetings in California, a routine occurrence. Little did anyone know the parting would be Hollingbery's last one with his Cougars. The program was in drydock in 1943–44, along with most others across the country. Upon its restart in 1945, Hollingbery found graduate manager (comparable to today's athletic director) Earl Foster unwilling to budge on salary terms.

"They offered him the job at the same salary of 1926," said Buster Hollingbery. "Their excuse was, they didn't know if there would be enough people coming to the games to pay his salary. That's baloney."

Thus ended the Babe's coaching era at WSU. He became a successful hops broker, moving to Yakima. He never coached full time again, but his son says his love for the school never wavered, and he might have stayed in Pullman indefinitely under better terms. "He was a football coach through and through," said his son.

This is how John McCallum, later a prolific author, summed up Hollingbery's exit in his *Evergreen* column in 1945: "The announcement today of his departure from the Cougar football scene fills us with utter disbelief and sorrow . . . besides the superb record he has piled up on the football field, it is universally agreed that Babe has had no peer among the coaches as a builder of character in the boys who have played under him . . . his kind will not pass this way again."

Babe Hollingbery finished with a 93–53–14 record. For that reason and others, McCallum may well have been right.

■　■　■

For decade upon decade, WSU made a cottage industry of trying to replicate that 1930 Rose Bowl season. It proved exceedingly difficult.

Phil Sarboe's 1945 team made a spirited run at it, with the returnees from World War II, going 6–2–1 but losing out to USC's 5–1. One of those holdovers was Giske, named AP All-Coast and winner of the team's Fred Bohler Award as most inspirational player. Giske had to be rerecruited—from a tuna boat, where he was doing commercial fishing with his dad off Astoria, Oregon.

"I was making about a thousand bucks a week," he said. But his dad implored him to finish school, and Giske knew the hard life of a fisherman. "It's no way to make a living," he said.

Forest Evashevski had a 7–3 team in 1951, but it finished in the middle of the Pacific Coast Conference standings. Then, in 1956, after some lean times under Al Kircher, the Cougars turned to a southern Californian who had just spent two years as a Washington assistant coach, Jim Sutherland.

He had some good teams in the late 1950s, and in fact his 1958 team came within a whisker of displacing Cal and going to the Rose Bowl. But the Cougars lost to the Bears, 34–14, and entered the final day of the season needing to beat Washington and have Cal lose to Stanford. WSU came through, 18–14, but Cal survived Stanford, 16–15.

What distinguished the eight-year Sutherland regime was some of the finest individual talent in school history. There was running back Keith Lincoln, ends Gail Cogdill and Hugh Campbell, and running back–defensive back Clancy Williams.

"I made a decision between, of all places, UCLA and here," said Lincoln, the school's retired alumni director. "I was a quarterback [in high school]. Red Sanders [UCLA coach] wanted me to be a tailback in the single wing. I came here because Jim Sutherland had developed a couple of All-American quarterbacks.

"My freshman year, Bob Newman was a junior, so Sutherland gave me the option of redshirting and being the starting quarterback for three years or being a running back. I decided to be a running back."

Lincoln, who blossomed late into a 6'1", 210-pound frame, had 1,501 career yards rushing at WSU and a punting average of 43.4 in 1959. He went on to greater renown as a back with the San Diego Chargers of the old American Football League, accounting for 349 yards total offense in one memorable playoff game.

But Sutherland's stock-in-trade was the pass, and he had two remarkable receivers in his tenure in Cogdill and Campbell. Cogdill had 252 yards receiving against Northwestern in 1958, a school record for 35 years, and went on to become NFL rookie of the year with the Detroit Lions.

"Just a really, really good athlete," Lincoln said. "He was about 6'2" or 6'3" and a solid 200 and could run like a deer and jump."

A lot of footballs—a WSU-career leading 176—came
Hugh Campbell's way.

What a Downer

Colorado once took advantage of an official's error to get an extra down—on which it scored the game-winning touchdown—to win a game at Missouri in its drive for a co-national title in 1990.

Long ago, WSU was on the short end of such a miscue, albeit with lesser repercussions. At Iowa in 1963, the Cougars came back from a 14–0 halftime deficit to tie it. Late in the game, they drove to the Hawkeye 24 and, with a strong wind at their backs, positioned themselves for a would-be game-winning field goal by Clete Baltes.

Alas, a Big Ten official got mixed up on an Iowa penalty and moved the down marker ahead, and after a third-down play by WSU to set up the kick, the Hawkeyes were allowed to take over. WSU coach Jim Sutherland protested and those in the press box yelped their consternation, but the decision stood, and the game ended in a 14–all tie.

Then there was the so-called "Phantom of the Palouse," Campbell, 6'0" and on the slight side. All he could do was catch: 176 balls in a three-year career (1960–62), easily still a WSU record. Campbell later won acclaim as a player, coach, and general manager in the Canadian Football League. "He was not going to get you with speed," said Lincoln, "but there wasn't a better set of hands to come along."

In 1964 Sutherland gave way to Bert Clark, from the Jim Owens–Dee Andros stable of Oklahoma-bred coaches. Clark's four-year regime wasn't particularly notable, except for two things: the 1965 season and the circumstances behind his departure two years later.

The 1965 Cardiac Kids were one of WSU's most intriguing and endearing teams, keyed by fullback Larry Eilmes, defensive tackle Wayne Foster, center Ron Vrlicak, defensive back Billy Gaskins, linebacker Dick Baird, and quarterback Tom Roth.

Seemingly, they didn't know how to play until it was close. They opened with victories on the road at Iowa and Minnesota, 7–0 and 14–13, respectively, each achieved in the closing seconds. After a loss to Idaho, they reeled off five straight wins, including an 8–7 stunner at Indiana, followed by a 10–8 nailbiter over Oregon State.

"We had a pretty high expectation to win," said halfback Ammon McWashington. "We were an older group."

The Indiana game was representative of much of the season. WSU didn't score for sixty minutes. But Indiana was called for pass interference on what would have been the game's last play, and on the replay Roth threw to receiver Doug Flansburg for 6 points, and the Cougars lined up to go for 2.

"All I remember is, we had three or four receivers to one side," said McWashington. "And we ran some picks." Roth threw to McWashington and the Cougars had their victory, scoring twice with no time on the clock.

Eerily, they had a chance to do almost exactly the same thing in the season's penultimate game at Arizona State. Scoring in the fourth quarter to narrow ASU's lead to 7–6, they went for two and

Bert Clark's 1965 Cardiac Kids played 'em close. Clark was ousted two years later.

threw again to McWashington. He got the ball across the goal line. But the Cougars had been whistled for delay of game, nullifying the play and giving ASU the victory.

"We got a bad call," said McWashington. "Usually with a delay of game, you would stop all play action."

WSU followed that with its only real clunker of the season, losing to Washington, 27–9, in Seattle. The "Cardiac Kids"—so named by *Spokane Chronicle* columnist Bob Johnson—finished 7–3.

Clark greased his own skids two years later. In the middle of a ten-game losing streak over two seasons, his team lost at Stanford, 31–10. Afterward, Clark was quoted as saying, "We should not even be playing in this conference . . . we were obviously outfought and what was even more discouraging, outcouraged."

Clark denied some of the comments, but reaffirmed one— that WSU "has the hardest recruiting problem in the conference because of our location." The coach found himself in hot water. Two days later, the school president, Glenn Terrell, issued a statement that the school expected to continue its conference affiliation "indefinitely." Not so its association with Clark, who was fired after the 1967 season, losing fifteen of his last twenty games in a four-year stint.

Meanwhile, the Rose Bowl drought was growing longer. It had stretched over five decades by the time Jim Walden's 1981 team made a serious run at it. The Cougars were coming off a 4–7 season. They had some excellent talent: quarterbacks Clete Casper and Ricky Turner (both of whom played in a two-quarterback system); running back Tim Harris; tight end Pat Beach; safety Paul Sorenson; defensive linemen Matt Elisara, Milford Hodge, and

Mike Walker; and linebacker Lee Blakeney, who would go on to put the career tackles record in the stratosphere, at 524.

The season-turning game came September 19 at Colorado, where the favored Buffs had a 10–0 lead with less than three minutes left. Then WSU scored twice, the latter one when Jeff Keller blocked a punt and Sorenson collected it and ran 43 yards for the game-winning score.

A little belief went a long way. A touchdown underdog the next week, WSU upended Arizona State and bolted to a 5–0 record. The Cougars were 6–0–1 before getting their comeuppance on Halloween, 41–17, at USC.

They were 8–1–1 when the moment of truth arrived. If the Cougars could knock off Washington in Seattle, the Rose Bowl was theirs. But they wouldn't catch the Huskies napping; a UW victory, combined with a USC win over UCLA, would put Washington in Pasadena. WSU had a 7–3 lead that looked like it would stand up until halftime. But with seconds remaining, UW receiver Paul Skansi got position on WSU cornerback Nate Bradley in the end zone and caught a 15-yard pass from Steve Pelluer. Washington locked down the Cougars the rest of the way for a 23–10 victory, and indeed, the Huskies got the Rose Bowl bid.

WSU consoled itself with its first bowl berth in fifty-one years, the Holiday, where its comeback against Brigham Young fell short in a 38–36 game. Outside Husky Stadium that November day, somebody was selling Cougar Rose Bowl shirts. They wouldn't be needed for awhile.

The Orphans

William Shakespeare, who never knew the Cougars of the mid- to late 1970s, once wrote, "Perseverance, dear my lord, keeps honor bright." Perseverance, fortitude, and, yes, a large helping of exasperation were the staples of WSU players who began at Washington State late in the Jim Sweeney era, surely figuring they would finish their college careers under his swaggering Irishness.

Little did they know. How could some of those players have guessed that by the time they saw a diploma, they would have experienced not only one new coach, but a couple of more in between? Who could have prepared them for a parade of mentors, giving rise to a rap on WSU for years as a place that couldn't keep a coach?

When he resigned as Cougar coach in 1975, the gregarious Jim Sweeney left a solid foundation.

First, there was Sweeney, who might have had the perfect temperament to coach the Cougars—indomitable, confident, ever the believer. Sam Jankovich, the former WSU and Miami athletic director who coached under Sweeney, recalls 1968, the first year of the regime, when the Cougars went 3–6–1 with 18 seniors but capped it with a 24–0 victory over Washington.

"Sweeney was going around the state, saying, 'The Huskies will never beat the Cougars again,'" Jankovich said. "I said, 'Jim, please take it easy. We don't have any players left.'" Sweeney's response, according to Jankovich: "We're going to outcoach 'em."

WSU went 7–4 in 1972, then skidded the next two years. But

cross-state rival Washington was struggling, and in the winter of 1973–74, Sweeney recruited a marvelous class. It included six players who were drafted by the NFL or Canadian Football League, people like Jack Thompson, Dan Doornink, Mike Levenseller, Brian Kelly, Eason Ramson, and Ken Greene.

One of Sweeney's assistants was the young Mike Price, who established himself as a dynamic recruiter. He staked out Thompson's home south of Seattle early on the signing date and beat Oregon to the punch, and Levenseller says Price conveniently dropped out of Sweeney's earshot when the head coach was concerned about "oversigning," made himself unavailable to be headed off, and signed Levenseller.

But by 1975, the eighth year of his tenure, Sweeney was growing weary. As he puts it, "I got tired of telling myself, and listening to myself, say we were gonna go to the Rose Bowl."

Conventional wisdom has it that a bizarre loss to Washington, in which two quirky plays brought the Huskies from a 27–14 deficit to a 28–27 win in the final three minutes, ended Sweeney's tenure. Sweeney's version is that he went to the home of the school president, Glenn Terrell, after a difficult 33–21 loss in the season's third game against California and told Terrell to begin thinking about Sweeney's successor.

Had he stayed, a lot of WSU history could have been different. Thompson, who had injured a knee in 1974 and thus fell a year behind his classmates in eligibility, remembers standing on the sidelines in that Washington game of '75 and plotting his transfer. "If Sweeney hadn't left, I was leaving," Thompson says. "Me and Levenseller [a wide receiver] and Don Schwartz [a linebacker]. I was rotting away on the bench. He didn't pass the ball,

'70, and Feeling Like It

Jim Sweeney, the gregarious former Washington State coach (1968–75), used to say that the rigors of the WSU job eventually wore him down. Surely, the year that chafed the most was 1970, which might go down as the worst in school history. The Cougars went 1–10 that season and during a four-game stretch of Pac-8 Conference games surrendered 232 points. But the really arresting statistic from that year is this: They had 36 passes intercepted, 11 more than their next-worst season.

Shortly, however, Sweeney engineered better days. He coached sixteen victories over the next three seasons and soon after recruited some of WSU's best talent—better, he says, than what he inherited in 1968.

"I had," he snorted, recalling his start at WSU, "about four Pac-8 players."

and I was a passing quarterback." Thompson talked about going south, to San Diego State. He and Levenseller also discussed teaming up at the University of Puget Sound. Imagine that pass-catch combination on the small-college level.

Then over Thanksgiving, the players were shocked to learn Sweeney was stepping down. "I guarantee you," said Sweeney, "I left it in a lot better shape than when I took it."

The new coach was Jackie Sherrill, a young assistant under Johnny Majors at Pittsburgh hired "out of the blue" by Terrell, according to Jankovich. Sherrill, he says, won out over WSU-bred Jerry Williams, then coaching in Canada, and assistant Lynn Stiles of UCLA.

In retrospect, the hire of Sherrill was perplexing, the importation of a Southerner coaching in the East whom everyone seemed to think would succeed Majors at Pitt when the opening materialized. It was Sherrill's first head-coaching job, and he was groping to find his way. His first order of business, Thompson says, was to run off "literally half the team" in the manner of his own college coach, the legendary Paul "Bear" Bryant at Alabama.

In winter drills, Thompson maintains, a pattern developed: He became a favorite whipping boy of Sherrill, getting paired in circuit drills with senior defensive tackle Tim Ochs, a high school wrestler who pounded on Thompson.

"The guys who stayed here," Thompson said, "were the crazy ones."

Levenseller remembers another practice he found distasteful. He and other top players would be sent off the field early to save themselves if a spring scrimmage was scheduled the next day. "We didn't want to go," Levenseller says. "It's a team thing. You didn't want to be separated. I argued with [Sherrill] about it. I got chewed out pretty good."

But for Thompson, Levenseller, Kelly, and anybody else who liked the ball in the air, something wonderful happened. Sherrill offered a 28-year-old assistant coach named Bob Leahy the offensive coordinator job, giving him more money and more responsibility than Majors could muster at Pitt. Leahy came west.

"I didn't like Bob Leahy," Thompson says. "I loved him. He was the best offensive coordinator I ever had."

Jackie Sherrill launched his head coaching career at WSU in 1976, but he was off to Pittsburgh after only a season.

Leahy had been a backup quarterback with the Pittsburgh Steelers, where he and Terry Bradshaw were rookie roommates. Also hired to the new staff was Otto Stowe, who had spent some time with the Dallas Cowboys and Miami Dolphins, and Leahy would pore over the playbooks Stowe brought with him. Sherrill gave Leahy free run of the offense, and Leahy ran with it.

"Nobody back then was spreading them out and going to the shotgun; that was unheard of," said Leahy, now at Louisiana-Monroe. "The neat thing was, Jackie was so involved with the defense, which really wasn't very good, and he just said, 'Hey, do whatever you have to do to score some points.' It was a fun deal."

Thompson believes Leahy was nothing less than a pioneer in offensive football on the West Coast.

"We were the first team in the Pac-10 (then the Pac-8) to go five wide receivers, no backs," Thompson says. "Guys in motion, spread offense. That also changed the fortunes of the position of quarterback at Washington State." Indeed, Thompson became the first of a recognized long legacy of quarterbacks at WSU, eventually including Mark Rypien, Timm Rosenbach, Drew Bledsoe, Ryan Leaf, and Jason Gesser.

Thompson's rise was rooted in the day Leahy began looking at film of the talent on hand. "I remember thinking, 'That Thompson kid can really throw it,'" Leahy said. "There was so much talent, at least offensive talent. Guys were so hungry and so coachable."

That might not be the recollection of Sherrill about Jack Thompson, who today is one of only two Cougars—the other is wunderkind center Mel Hein (1928–30)—to have had a number retired. "Jackie," says Thompson, "didn't like me."

Strong-armed Jack Thompson is one of only two Cougar football players to have his number retired.

Maybe it had something to do with those first winter drills. Or maybe it stemmed from that day in Minneapolis in 1976, when, as Thompson puts it, "I kind of snuck into a game." Thompson, a future number four overall pick in the 1979 NFL draft, was still languishing as a reserve quarterback behind John Hopkins and Wally Bennett. As Thompson recalls, he ducked into the game when there was a brief equipment malfunction. Leahy had called a running play, but as Thompson got to the line of scrimmage, he saw the Gophers crowding the line of scrimmage. In his first snap in anger in Sherrill's regime, he called an audible to a pass.

Out he came, to find Sherrill "screaming bloody murder" at him. When Sherrill stopped, Leahy barked at Thompson over the headset. "I knew that, for all intents and purposes, I was kicked off the team," Thompson said.

They came to the locker room at halftime. Thompson was wondering how he was going to explain to his father that he'd been booted. Instead, Leahy approached him and delivered a shocker: Would he be ready to start the second half? Hopkins had dinged a knee escaping a rush and wasn't available. Thompson performed adequately in the second half of a 28–14 loss that dropped the Cougars to 0–2. The next week, in a 35–26 loss at Wisconsin, Hopkins returned to start, but Thompson came in shortly thereafter, and the job was now his.

Victories were scarce. WSU came from behind to beat Oregon on the road, 23–22, and downed Oregon State, 29–24, the next week. At California the next Saturday, the Cougars dug themselves a big hole before Thompson began leading them back on a day that marked the next volatile chapter in the Sherrill-Thompson relationship.

WSU fought back to a 23–22 deficit and in the final seconds had a two-point conversion attempt that would win the game. But the Cougars missed a blitz pickup, Burl Toler leveled Thompson, and Cal survived to win by a point.

As he trotted off the field, Thompson was accosted by Sherrill, who was livid. He grabbed Thompson's facemask, blamed him for the defeat and exhausted most of the expletives in his vocabulary.

"I said, 'I've had it,'" Thompson recalls. "'I'm out of here.'"

"Come back here, son," ordered Sherrill.

"Tell that to my dad," said the father-fearing Thompson. "He'll tell you who's my father." With seconds remaining, Thompson left the field. He reached the locker room, and the first person he encountered was Leahy, who was unaware of the dustup on the sideline.

"Great game," Leahy said.

"Thanks, coach," Thompson replied. "I think I just quit the team."

Then Sherrill walked in, and everything blew up. In a towel room at Cal's venerable Memorial Stadium, he and Thompson had what the quarterback calls a "come-to-Jesus" meeting, screaming at each other. Thompson said he was tired of being the whipping boy.

Somehow, Thompson seemed to win Sherrill over, but it would hardly matter. Washington was next—the Huskies would win 51–32 to finish a 3–8 season for the Cougars—and Jankovich says that before that week he knew something was up. "We knew Jackie was gonna go, just with his attitude alone," Jankovich says.

Indeed, Majors, whose Pitt team won the 1976 national championship, would shortly be off to Tennessee, and Sherrill, as everybody had seemed to expect when he took the Washington

State job, was the person named to replace him.

Sherrill's twelve-month tenure was tumultuous, right to the finish. Levenseller remembers a team meeting at which Sherrill was announcing his goodbye, when George Yarno, the big defensive tackle who has done two assistant's stints at the school, stood up and snarled, "Get the hell out."

"I'll never forget it," said Levenseller, who had a year of eligibility left to Yarno's two. "I never saw Jackie sheepish in my entire time here with him. That was the one moment where he didn't have control of the situation. Jackie got out of here, and I never saw him again."

At times, Sherrill had been monstrously difficult for the players, a first-year head coach who was quintessential Bear Bryant. On the other hand, in Leahy, the WSU offensive players had been introduced to a vibrant new way of doing things. Referring to Sherrill, Levenseller said, "I don't know that he ever became part of the climate, and I don't mean weather. We played hard for him, and I think he respected us because of that. I never would have played pro football if it hadn't been for him. I've always known that."

"There was something about Jackie," said Thompson, referring to a winning aura. "He had an air about him. He had rings and stuff like that. It was a stretch to see him staying in Pullman a long time."

But it was Leahy who really pulled at Thompson's heartstrings. They were so close, Leahy would name a son Jack Thomas Leahy. "I cried like a baby when Bob Leahy said goodbye," Thompson said.

Unfortunately for the orphans, the hellos and goodbyes were becoming a way of life.

A Search for Stability

Unlike Jack Thompson, Sam Jankovich wasn't crying, he was boiling. As he sought out another head football coach, the WSU athletic director knew the job might seem further devalued with Sherrill's sudden departure.

Jankovich went looking primarily for top assistant coaches, one of whom was Mal Moore of Alabama. Moore would later be the 'Bama athletic director who hired Mike Price in 2002. Even prying Moore away for an interview was no easy trick, Jankovich learned. He had to go through the iconic Bryant first.

"Bear [initially] wouldn't let him come [for an interview]," Jankovich said. Affecting a deep, gravelly Bear voice, Jankovich said, "Listen, we're recruiting, working hard. He can catch a red-eye, be there in six hours, then get his butt back here and recruit."

Frazzled by an all-night flight, Moore didn't wow anybody, Jankovich remembers. "Poor Mal got off the plane a nervous wreck," Jankovich said. "He's a great guy. But he didn't do a good job." Instead, Jankovich targeted a defensive backs coach at Nebraska, Warren Powers.

"I really thought Warren had a touch nobody else had," Jankovich said. "I think a secondary coach, a great secondary coach, they see things nobody else does."

Thompson and Yarno found themselves on the search committee helping Jankovich. Thompson remembers Powers as a better fit for Pullman, a more folksy character than Sherrill. He was somebody who seemed like he might stay.

"I remember asking him the question: 'We can't afford to have you come in and leave like Coach Sherrill did. Tell me your thoughts,'" Thompson recalls.

"I'm here, I'm anchored," Thompson remembers Powers saying.

Powers, in the automobile business in St. Louis since the early 1990s, recalls being flattered by the interview, not necessarily thinking he would win the job. But he got it. "It takes a little wind out of you," he said. "Once they offered it to me, I said, 'Wow!'"

The first order of business, of course, was putting together a staff. That was of great importance in particular to Thompson, who hoped fervently Leahy would be invited to stay.

It wasn't to be. In an ironic twist, Leahy wasn't invited to stay by Powers and was beckoned to Pitt by Sherrill, who left the majority of his WSU staff looking for jobs.

"He left all those guys stranded," said Leahy. "The only guy he was taking back to Pitt was me, and I didn't want to go. I had to go back. Now I'd been coaching four years total, I'm going to be offensive coordinator at Pittsburgh, the national champs, and I didn't even want to go."

Leahy had little choice. He recalls his first meeting with Powers, which wasn't really a meeting. "He gave me a token interview," Leahy says. "As soon as I walked in there, he said, 'Hey, Bob, you're one of Jackie's guys, so I don't want to do anything with you here.'"

Leahy recalls going to a basketball game with Thompson after he learned he wasn't going to be retained. "There were really some tears on that night," Leahy said.

The postscript on Leahy is that he stayed with Sherrill only one more year. "Jackie and I had our differences, and I walked out on him," Leahy says. That led him back to the West Coast, where he worked for Roger Theder at Cal, and in a bit of historical trivia, carpooled with three future NFL head coaches from that staff: Al Saunders, Gunther Cunningham, and Dom Capers.

Meanwhile, Jankovich was busy brainstorming a contract with Powers that made national headlines. He came up with the idea of the "buyout" clause so prevalent in today's coaching agreements: tying the coach to the school for a specified time with a provision requiring a payment if he leaves the program before then.

Part of a revolving door of coaches in the 1970s, Warren Powers was gone to Missouri after only one year at WSU.

What is commonplace today was unprecedented then. But the Cougars were now on a third coach in three seasons. "Needless to say, I didn't have any idea I was going to be there one year," Powers said. "I was totally engulfed in the program. The kids were very buoyant. They rebounded [from the coaching change] and accepted us very well."

When Powers came west, one of his assistant coaching colleagues at Nebraska, Monte Kiffin—who had been a candidate at WSU—joined Lou Holtz's staff at Arkansas. One of Powers's first acts as WSU coach was to visit Holtz at Arkansas regarding offense and head coaching.

"I got some great ideas from Lou," Powers says.

One of those notions wasn't exactly what Thompson wanted to hear, but Powers was honest. "He said in the interview, 'We're not going to pass as much as you did; we've got to be balanced in order to win,'" Thompson said. "'But when we do pass, we're going to be more efficient.'"

Powers didn't run a boot camp quite the way Sherrill did. For one, he had a more veteran team, and it clearly wasn't a squad without talent.

"Warren was one of my favorite guys," says Levenseller. "He had the personality that really fit that group of seniors. He treated us like adults. His personality was one that he could get us to do what he wanted. Warren brought in a good staff, good guys. We were a little bit further established now."

As luck would have it, the very first game on the schedule was Nebraska. Not only did the Cougars have their own infiltrator into Cornhusker intelligence in Powers, he had brought with him some staff members. Probably no program in the country knew Nebraska like Washington State.

Not only that, Powers had brought to his staff Jim Walden. He had not only coached at Nebraska in 1971–72, but he had been an assistant at the University of Miami in 1976, when the

Hurricanes had a hard-fought 17–9 loss to the Huskers.

"I understood Tom," Walden said, referring to Tom Osborne, the Nebraska head coach. "When I came out here, I wasn't intimidated by Nebraska."

As spring practice 1977 materialized, Walden began to like what he saw. "I knew we had something pretty special," Walden said. "A quarterback, running back, five pretty good receivers."

To hear Thompson tell it, Powers's choreography of the appearance in Lincoln was nothing short of brilliant. "He had pictures of the Nebraska stadium in the hallway," Thompson said. "He described how it was going to be, how everywhere you look, it's going to be red. 'Just get to know it now.'"

Powers remembers being reluctant to exchange spring-game films with Osborne, figuring it was the Huskers who were at a knowledge deficit. He decided to do it but showed Nebraska almost nothing in the game.

Over the summer Walden, studying Nebraska film, noticed something consistent about the Husker defense. On offenses' first downs inside the Nebraska red zone, the Huskers blitzed, feeling they "had to make something happen."

"Over and over and over, I saw that," Walden says.

Powers worried a bit about the heartland heat for a September 10 opener, but he was holding all the cards.

"I knew their defense, I knew their secondary because I had coached 'em," he said. "I knew what hurt us when I was there, and we had a real strong passing game. Tom [Osborne] didn't know a lot about Jack, didn't know how good the guy was."

Levenseller remembers the Cougars' charter aircraft circling Memorial Stadium in Lincoln before landing as Nebraska practiced. It was an audacious way to announce the arrival of a 17-point underdog.

But Saturday would be the Cougars' day, in one of the biggest upsets in school history. True to the film Walden had watched, the Huskers blitzed Thompson, who threw two slants to Kelly for touchdowns. WSU won, 19–10.

"I said this many times after we played the game: No disrespect to Nebraska, but I beat them in my mind a hundred times because of Coach Powers," Thompson said. "Yes, we were nervous, but once we got into the game, we just kind of kicked into automatic pilot."

You begin to understand the suicide scheduling WSU was undertaking in those days by looking at 1976–77. In 1976, the Cougars started at Kansas, at Minnesota, and at Wisconsin. In 1977, they followed Nebraska with successive trips to Michigan State, Kansas, and USC. They didn't play their first home game until October 8. But they carved out a 6–5 season. Then the unthinkable began happening again.

Late in October Walden made an offer on a house. He liked Pullman, seeing it as a good place to raise kids. One day Powers asked him to stop by his home to let Walden know he was getting into the picture for the head coaching job at Missouri, his alma mater.

"I was totally confused," Walden says. "I was under the impression Warren had made a commitment to the Washington State people. I understood the attraction, but it didn't make it any easier. I didn't take the news well."

Nor did anybody else. Players like Levenseller and Kelly were now done, but Thompson, who had become the Cougars' meal ticket, still had a senior year to play. "Warren Powers still ticks me off, what he did," Thompson says. "Why'd he ever take the stupid job?"

Thompson says President Terrell was on the west side of the state, making a last-ditch appeal to keep Powers. Terrell promised to call Thompson hourly to tell him how the evening was going.

In mid-evening, Thompson got a call from Walden, who wanted an update from Thompson, no matter how late. Thompson heard from Terrell late that night, informing him Powers was gone, and Thompson relayed the news to Walden.

"I want to get together," Walden said.

"I'm thinking he's going to say tomorrow morning," Thompson said. "He says, 'Right now.'"

In the dead of night, the star quarterback and coach-to-be met in front of the old St. Thomas More church building above downtown Pullman. They went from there to a restaurant in Moscow, and Walden let him know he would be throwing his hat into the ring for the vacancy.

Powers? Jankovich tagged him with the first buyout in college-football history, something like $75,000. "Sam Jankovich had been so great to me," Powers said. "It was really the toughest decision I've ever had to make. I'm sure I made a lot of enemies out there. We were just getting started. We had talked about the program a lot, sold the program to the people, and then to pull up and leave like that, it was like a turncoat deal."

The belief among WSU people is that Powers's wife pushed him to return to his roots, but he says that was overstated. "She was very good—she said, 'I'm happy at either place,'" he insisted. "It would have been a lot easier if she had pushed me."

Retiring Sorts

Only two football players in WSU history have had their numbers retired, and although some of the Cougars' best football has been played in the past quarter-century, neither came very recently.

Mel Hein (1927–31), widely considered the best center ever to play the game, was the first Cougar so honored. He was an All-American at Washington State, a fixture with the New York Giants for fifteen years, and later a member of both the college and NFL halls of fame.

Half a century later came Jack Thompson (1974–78), the strong-armed quarterback who passed for 7,818 yards, then an NCAA career record. Thompson is one of the most recognizable Cougars, a tireless spokesman and advocate for the school.

With recent standouts like Drew Bledsoe and Ryan Leaf, there have been suggestions of adding to the Hein-Thompson duo, but no action has been taken. A school publicist says there is no standard policy governing the retirement of numbers.

Jankovich, of course, turned to Walden to recast Washington State football once again. It was a bit of good news that Thompson heard in an unlikely place. Seems that Thompson, the "Throwin' Samoan," had gotten a letter from Hollywood, interested in auditioning him for a key role in *The Hurricane*, a 1979 remake of a 1937 film that combined disaster and romance in the South Seas. Initially, Thompson thought it was a hoax but then

After a flurry of coaching changeovers in the 1970s, Jim Walden brought stability to the position in a nine-year tenure (1978–86).

learned it was real. The filmmakers had seen his photograph in a Los Angeles newspaper.

"Once they met me, they realized two things," said Thompson. "One, I was too big for the role, and two, I looked too old. I was supposed to look like a sixteen-year-old."

In Los Angeles, Thompson got a hurried call from Walden, telling him he needed to return so they could announce Thompson was staying for his senior year. The whole affair was fitting. By then Thompson probably figured he had spent the past four years in a movie.

Thus, in the late summer of 1978, when the league's "Sky-writers" came through for the first tour of the league as a ten-team entity, Walden hung a cardboard sign around his neck, meant to head off the obvious question: "Yes, I plan to honor my contract."

He did, and more, staying nine seasons. Walden remembers that first, edgy meeting with a jaded team. "I don't know of very many coaches who walked into a more hostile room," he said. "I wasn't going to do this phony-baloney 'You'll like me.' I said, 'I'm delighted I'm your head coach, I'm dreadfully sorry Warren Powers is not your head coach. On the other hand, don't try to take advantage of the situation, because you'll get no sympathy from me.'"

After starting 3–0, Walden's first club finished only 4–6–1. But three years later he had a Holiday Bowl team that played in WSU's first post-season game in fifty-one years. By then, the "Orphans" of the recent past were gone to other callings, perhaps a bit more callous but most of them better for having shown the resilience to survive four coaches in four seasons. They were always having to adapt, always having to prove themselves all over again, but maybe it made them better.

"The fan base, in a weird way, commiserated," Thompson says. "They empathized with the plight of those kids at Washington State that stayed. They represented something pure—kids who had great talent and stayed at Washington State. A lot of those guys today are fondly remembered."

Return to the Wheat Fields

Not long after he became athletic director at Washington State in 1976, Sam Jankovich had a brainstorm. The Cougars, with the smallest football stadium in the Pac-10 at about 27,000, would dig down, tear out the track, and extract some 16 feet from inside Martin Stadium. Voilà, another 12,400 seats, something to bring the Cougars into the twentieth century. The notion was met with skepticism, even derision, from civic and campus leaders, some of whom called it a project to create a hole in the ground.

Apparently they weren't farsighted enough to visualize the day when WSU students would tear out the goal posts, ferry them a mile downtown, and deposit them in the Palouse River. Nor did they foresee an afternoon that, years later, would cause ex-football coach Jim Walden to say, "Whether it's the biggest thing that ever happened in my life in coaching, I don't know. I'll leave it pretty high. I do know, it was one of the biggest things to happen to Washington State University."

This was the setup: Historically, the Cougars had been viewed with a jaded eye in some quarters of the Pacific-8 Conference. Pullman was a hard place to travel to, it had the coldest fall and winter weather, and because of the modest size of Martin Stadium, the visiting paycheck was relatively skimpy.

Because of that stadium size, it became de rigueur for the Cougars to play many of their games in Spokane, 80 miles north, at 36,000-seat Joe Albi Stadium. It was a tradition that took hold in the earliest years of the program, was reinstated with a couple of games in 1942, and was brought out of mothballs again with the Washington game of 1950.

It was in the 1950s that custom took a firm foothold, one that surely contributed to some desultory seasons at Washington State in the next three decades. Three of the power programs in what is now the Pac-10—USC, UCLA, and Washington—held out for the WSU home games to be in Spokane rather than Pullman, diluting the home-field advantage and making for easier travel on the visitors.

The arrangement included everything but a ransom note. Imagine Nebraska playing two or three home games a year in Omaha. Or Michigan journeying over to Detroit a couple of times a season. Or Tennessee playing host in Nashville, not Knoxville. Today, fans recognize Washington State as a difficult place for the visitor to win. As a program, it used to be hard for Washington State to win, simply because it didn't play very many games in Pullman.

As athletic director in the 1970s and 1980s, Sam Jankovich oversaw the expansion of Martin Stadium and brought the Apple Cup back to Pullman.

Enter Jankovich and his harebrained idea. At a cost of $2.5 million, some of it donated, the project took flight, and by 1979 the new stadium was ready. The track stadium was bumped just to the north, which in turn moved the baseball field a bit east. A few years before that, another project came to fruition eight miles across the state border. The University Inn was built, a 173-room motel in neighboring Moscow, a bigger, more attractive facility than existed anywhere in the two college towns that are home to WSU and the University of Idaho.

"It sounds kind of stupid," says Jankovich. "But it gave us much better accommodation of the teams. With that motel and the expansion of the stadium, there was no reason they could not play us."

The last time UCLA had played in Pullman was 1955, when the Bruins, coming off a national-championship year, hung a 55–0 loss on the Cougars. In an interrupted series, WSU had then played UCLA seven times in Spokane, losing every one—often badly.

The inaugural game in the refurbished Martin Stadium came against UCLA on October 13, 1979. Whether it was the venue, who knows, but the Cougars prevailed. It must have been worth something; WSU was a 15½-point underdog. "Glory be, we won 17–14," Walden says. "It was a wonderful day."

But now came the acid test: convincing the Huskies to play in the confines of Pullman, not Spokane. You had to go all the way back to 1954 to find the last time Washington had ventured to the Palouse country. In the intervening thirteen meetings in Spokane, Washington had a big 10–3 advantage. A chasm was growing between the two programs. Starting in 1974, Washington won eight straight in a series that had become known as the Apple Cup. In the last three games in Spokane—WSU's nominal home—the Huskies had scored at least 30 points in their victories.

Washington had begun flourishing under legendary coach Don James, going to Rose Bowls with some regularity, including the 1981 season, when a victory over WSU in Seattle prevented the long-suffering Cougars from a trip to Pasadena.

Jankovich still recalls the fateful phone call with Mike Lude, the militaristic athletic director at Washington, when they discussed the site of the 1982 game.

"We're playing in Spokane," said Lude.

"It's the home team's decision," Jankovich protested.

"We're not gonna do it," Lude insisted.

"That's up to you," Jankovich retorted. "We'll be in Pullman, and you'll be in Spokane. If you don't show up, we win, and you lose."

The Huskies showed up but only grudgingly. Everything about this game smelled of upset—everything except the point spread, which was 17.

"We would never have wanted to play the game in Pullman if it was up to us," James told the *Seattle Times* in 2002. Washington had a gaudy 9–1 record. The Huskies were quarterbacked by Tim Cowan and featured running back Jacque Robinson, who had been most valuable player in the previous Rose Bowl. They had dependable receiver Paul Skansi, an all-league linebacker in Mark Stewart, and an All-American placekicker in Chuck Nelson, who had made 28 straight field goals.

The Huskies were positioned for a fourth Rose Bowl in six seasons under James. A week earlier they had won a big road game at contending Arizona State, 17–13, nosing ahead of ASU in a competitive Pac-10 race. All they had to do was overcome a struggling Washington State team and their ticket to Pasadena was punched.

WSU was laboring through a 2–7–1 season, having expected bigger things but enduring a year marked by injuries. The Cougars had young players who would be future stars—defensive linemen like Keith Millard, Erik Howard, and Milford Hodge—plus some capable offensive weapons in dual quarterbacks Clete Casper and Ricky Turner, as well as running back Tim Harris.

By November 20, some of those injured players began to make it back. "I had had a shoulder problem for most of the year," said Casper. "We were finally starting to get the same guys on the field we'd played with (in 1981) and had so much success with."

For his part, Walden believed he had the Huskies right where he wanted them. "Our whole staff felt we had a great chance," he said. "We didn't think Washington, as good as they were, knew how hard our guys were going to play. And I had a better football team than Don (James) thought I did."

Walden knew this was the kind of setting that would unnerve James, who was the ultimate detail guy. It used to be said that the Husky coach knew exactly how many minutes it would take him on Sunday morning to drive from taping his TV highlight show to his office on Montlake Boulevard, where he could immerse himself in preparation.

For this game, James wouldn't know the nuances of the stadium, which way the wind might tend to blow at a certain time. He didn't know about the reliability of the team motel, whether

Tackling Machine

The signature of Washington State football has been its offense, but it's a defensive record that figures to stand for a long time. Lee Blakeney, a 6'0", 234-pound linebacker from Concord, California, amassed 524 tackles from 1980 to 1984, putting him far ahead of number two Anthony McClanahan's 440 on the career list.

"He had a great understanding of what we were trying to get done," said Jim Walden, Blakeney's coach. "And he had an unbelievable ability to use what he had. He was a wrestler, and linebacking wrestlers always seem to have an understanding of how to stay on their feet."

Walden stationed Blakeney at outside linebacker on the weak side. He responded with 129 tackles as a freshman and topped that by one as a sophomore. Just before the 1982 season began, Blakeney was felled by a knee injury that sidelined him for the year. But he came back with 112 tackles as a junior and finished with 153 in 1984.

Said Walden, "Lee just knew where he needed to be."

the pregame meal would be on time, and these things were important.

"I knew him enough to know these were uncharted waters," said Walden, "and it was going to be a distraction to him. I also knew he didn't have a single football player on his team that had a single bit of respect for our team."

Casper says there were newspaper advertisements that week—so the Cougars were told, anyway—promoting travel packages for a UW appearance in the Rose Bowl. The Washington State players were already riled at the recollection of how the Huskies had deprived them in 1981 of their first Rose Bowl appearance since 1930. Washington's practices for the game only seemed to confirm James's worries. "It was like pulling teeth all week," he said.

Meanwhile, on game's eve, Walden revealed a bit of his own strategy to Casper, who had been alternating with Turner in a two-quarterback system. Casper, 6'3" and 192 pounds, brought more polished passing to the offense, while the skittery Turner, 5'11", 178 and a year younger, could be a nightmare to defenses as a runner.

"Coach Walden suggested I was going to be able to start and play the whole game as a senior, which was kind of fun," said Casper. "I really hadn't had the opportunity in my career to play the whole game."

Game day brought a brisk thirty-seven degrees, showers, and some stiff breezes. When the Cougars emerged for pregame warm-ups, Martin Stadium was electric. "The atmosphere was beyond anything I'd seen then and since," Walden says. "It was almost like the students came at five o'clock [in the morning]. For the first time ever, the place was packed."

The teams parried ineffectively for several possessions. Then Robinson burst for 36 yards to the WSU 37. Four plays later, Cowan threw a 24-yard touchdown strike to Anthony Allen, and the Huskies had a 7–0 lead.

A fumble by WSU tight end Vince Leighton set the Huskies

up early in the second quarter, and they drove twelve plays before the automatic Nelson connected on a 21-yard field goal, making it 10–0.

On the Cougars' fourth possession, they began to give evidence of one of the game's keys: an ability to run on the Huskies. Washington had recently been vulnerable on the ground, having surrendered 462 yards rushing in its previous three games.

A fifteen-play, 73-yard drive that took up almost half the second quarter brought WSU within 10–7. In the middle of it, Harris carried six straight times for 37 yards. That momentum was quickly blunted, however, when the Huskies marched smartly from their own 19 to a touchdown in eight plays, Cowan throwing on third-and-eight to Allen again for a 16-yard touchdown.

So at halftime there wasn't much to portend an upset; the Huskies were both running and throwing on the Cougars, amassing 235 yards of total offense. But shortly into the second half, the mounting pressure seemed to weigh on the Huskies. On their second series, Skansi, at the UW 28, fumbled, and WSU inside linebacker Ben Carrillo recovered. There was all sorts of karma attached to the play, as it was Skansi's first career fumble, and in the Pasadena–deciding game a year earlier, it had been Skansi's unusual touchdown catch late in the half that turned the game in Washington's favor.

After Skansi's fumble the Cougars capitalized quickly. Matthews's 13-yard sweep on the first play helped set up Casper's 6-yard scoring pass to Mike Peterson. More irony there. Peterson was from Spokane, the place the Huskies wanted to be on this day.

In short order, Washington contributed another key mistake. Senior tailback Dennis Brown juggled the ensuing kickoff, and

Get That License Number

Washington State coaches from Jim Sweeney to Jim Walden to Mike Price have had a reputation for the colorful phrase. Personality has seemingly been part of the job description in out-of-the-way Pullman.

Perhaps no coach has unleashed a better string of zingers than Walden in the days after his 1986 team lost to California, 31–21. "I could wind up robots and get the same effort," Walden told a Spokane booster group. "I went into the season thinking there were six teams on our schedule that we were as good as, or maybe a little better than, and five others that would be the difference between jeeps and tanks. I don't mind getting run over by a tank. But we just got run over this week by a damn moped."

Walden's early-season frustration proved meaningful. After five losses to end the season, he resigned as head coach after nine years and took the same job at Iowa State.

---

after he could return only to the 5, the Huskies had to punt from their 11. That set up WSU in Washington territory at the 48, and the Cougars were now into it. They ran the ball straight at the Huskies, and with the help of a pass-interference call, found themselves with a first-and-goal at the UW 7.

Via e-mail from Prague, where he runs a venture-capital fund, WSU's standout guard Dan Lynch remembers the call: 41 Trap, a handoff to Harris behind Lynch after a fake sweep right.

"When the ball was hiked, I took a false step, expecting the defensive tackle to bite on the sweep so I could take him across the hole," Lynch remembers. "Instead, he jumped left, so I moved towards his upfield shoulder to pin him outside the hole. The combination of the two events [i.e., everyone moving right but the defensive tackle pinned left] created a massive hole, which Tim Harris used to just walk into the end zone."

Suddenly, the Cougars were ahead 21–17 with 4:43 left in the third quarter. Game on. The Huskies responded immediately with a methodical drive of fifteen plays, but the Cougars stiffened, and Nelson toed his NCAA-record thirtieth straight field goal from 37 yards, bringing Washington within a point.

Early in the fourth quarter, WSU had a prime opportunity to add to the lead at the UW 39, but Casper threw an interception to cornerback Ray Horton at the Husky 11 with 9:18 left. There, the Huskies began a long drive, and it's safe to say the majority of those watching and listening figured it would be a winning one. They reached the WSU 16, and with 4:35 left, Nelson lined up for a 33-yard field goal. The ball sailed over an upright—wide right.

The miss has become a piece of Apple Cup lore, something Nelson is ribbed about regularly by Cougars, one of the few skeletons in a sterling college and pro career. A chunk of the goal post was converted into a trophy with an engraved inscription in the WSU football offices. Nelson has contended the kick was close enough that he might have gotten the call at home.

"It wasn't that close," Casper insists. "It gets closer every year, according to Chuck."

"I'm not sure there's ever been a greater, more accurate kicker," Walden says. "The saddest thing for Chuck Nelson is,

WSU was given little chance in the 1982 Apple Cup, but when it was over, Jim Walden got a lift off the field.

he's had to carry that thing with him. Look at how many games he won."

It was left for the Cougars to force a sack of Cowan at the UW 28 with 2:05 left, resulting in freshman John Traut's 37-yard field goal with 56 seconds showing, insurance for a 24–20 upset. WSU students wrenched down the goal posts, marshaled them downtown and deposited them in the Palouse River.

The Huskies were left with a bid to the Aloha Bowl, where they nipped Maryland for a ten-victory season. Still, James said, "I think that was the most disappointing loss in my eighteen years. We lost so much that year, the chance to go to the Rose Bowl, the chance to three-peat. I couldn't sleep for two weeks."

The day seemed to change the rivalry forever, signaling that the Cougars would be a threat to Washington. Indeed, they won the next two games in Seattle, in 1983 again denying the Huskies a Rose Bowl berth.

Walden believes there was even a greater impact, both academic and athletic. Focus was brought to the WSU campus, and auxiliary events grew around the game. "If you were playing in Spokane," he says, "you didn't do any of that. It did more for the university than people will ever know. I may be glamorizing it up a little. But I don't think so."

The Rampaging Rueben

Late in October of 1984, they turned Rueben Mayes loose. He had been a good running back until those two weeks but not spectacular. Suddenly, though, in a span of eight days, Mayes was scintillating, a record-breaking bolt of electricity who trained the spotlight not only on himself but on Washington State.

When it was over, when he had run for 573 yards in two games—still unsurpassed in Pac-10 history—even his classmates in another sport were moved to give him a standing ovation. He was the sort of individual who deserved it. His coach, Jim Walden remembers him as one of those guys just delighted to be there, whether it was rolling out to attend an 8:00 A.M. class or perform dreary ball-security drills.

Referring to Mayes's demeanor, Walden says, "Everything we did was just a joy." If Mayes ranks as one of WSU's best players in history, he also must stand as one of its unlikeliest recruits. He wasn't from the teeming talent pool in southern California, or the drizzle of western Washington, but from the improbable farm country of North Battleford, Saskatchewan.

His town was a little bigger than 10,000 people, and as a child Rueben was slender and very fast. He ran world-class times in the 55 meters indoors as a high school competitor. But his passion lay elsewhere. "My dream," he says, "was to be an NFL player."

He recalls, as a junior high schooler, watching the high school team. A cousin, small but quick, was a key player. "Rueben, if you work hard like that, you can play high school football," his mother told him.

"I'm going to play NFL football, Mom," her son replied. "You don't even know it yet."

The high school coach's name was Don Hodgins, and he knew how to exploit the running game. One time, North Battleford was playing the city kids from Regina, and Mayes slipped on the turf. A defender snarled at him, "You ain't any good." Mayes brushed him off, and his team ran the ball at will and won in a blowout.

His recruitment was understated, to say the least, mostly limited to some small schools in North Dakota and the breadth of Canada. In his native country, he heard the warning more than once: "Rueben, you shouldn't go down to the States. You'll get lost in the crowd."

But there was a game side to Mayes that told him to give big-time American collegiate football a chance. Hugh Campbell, the WSU receiving great who became a Canadian professional coach, knew about Mayes and got in touch with the Cougar staff. WSU became his only recruiting visit. He liked the school, and it seemed to like Mayes back.

"I remember staying in Streit Hall," he says. "There was a floor party, all these girls. I'd never been exposed to anything like that in my life." He got lost one night trying to find his way back to the dorm, but it didn't dull the experience. He ate breakfast one morning at the old Cougar Café in downtown Pullman, and as he remembers it, another recruit dropped off WSU's list and the coaches offered him a scholarship. He took it.

Mayes had a good freshman year in 1982, then had a shoulder injury that dimmed his 1983 season. The next year, the Cougars had future Super Bowl MVP Mark Rypien at quarterback and Kerry Porter alongside Mayes at running back.

There was little that augured greatness on the afternoon of October 20, 1984, at Stanford Stadium. Porter was injured and the Cougars were 2–4.

For the better part of forty minutes on a clear, sixty-degree day, the Cougars were a mess. As Walden puts it, "We're in the process of playing one of our top five worst games I could possibly have coached." Under first-year coach Jack Elway, a former assistant at WSU, Stanford had a mediocre team that would finish 5–6. No matter; it was making roadkill of the Cougars, leading 28–7 at halftime and then scoring on two of its first three drives of the third quarter for a 42–14 lead with 5:38 left in the period.

Walden swears he looked across the sideline and saw some Stanford starters unraveling tape from their wrists, content to let the Cardinal reserves play out the string. Dan Lynch, WSU's standout guard, remembers going to the far end of the sideline, looking up at the scoreboard, and saying in exasperation to no one in particular, "What do we have to do?" In that moment of despair, he couldn't have known there was an easy answer: Get the ball in Rueben Mayes's hands.

What took place next was twenty minutes of the most stunning, extraordinary, explosive football WSU has ever generated. As the third quarter waned, Mayes took a handoff from Rypien on a draw play and charged 39 yards for a touchdown to finish a quick, 72-yard drive. That made it 42–21.

With seventy seconds left in the quarter, WSU began another drive, having stopped Stanford's three running plays. On the first play of the fourth quarter, Mayes ran for 16 yards over left tackle, and the smallest germ of hope was beginning to grow in the WSU huddle.

"Our defense was beginning to come together and hold them," Mayes says. "We were just clicking. Mark was hitting some short passes to John Marshall and Rick Chase, and we were running the ball better."

Less than two minutes into the last quarter, Rypien had scored on a 6-yard keeper, and it was 42–27 after the extra point

No back in Pac-10 history has rushed for more yards (573) than Rueben Mayes did in two remarkable games in 1984.

misfired. "I'm looking over [at the Stanford sideline]," Walden says, "and the trainer's got all their guys, and they're re-taping. Jack's screaming at 'em, because he didn't tell 'em to take the tape off."

Then came one of the game's pivotal plays. Ron Collins, WSU's free safety, remembers Stanford having some of its "hands" team members in the game, suspecting an onside kick. But the Cougars kicked deep, Kevin Scott misjudged the ball and fumbled, and Kevin Thomasson recovered for the Cougars at the 5-yard line. One quick pitch to Mayes, and WSU was within a touchdown at 42–35.

Now time wasn't really a factor. The teams exchanged punts, and WSU held Stanford for a third straight series, pushing the Cardinal back 8 yards in three plays to its own 17. Taking over at its 43, WSU suffered a 10-yard sack against Rypien, but on the next play the Cougar junior floated a screen pass to Mayes. He spotted a crease, split it, and raced 53 yards for the score, and when John Traut added the conversion with 5:35 remaining, it was knotted at 42.

Once again, the defense arose. On Stanford's second play from its 25, Collins made his second of three interceptions. After his 13-yard runback and a clipping penalty, WSU had the ball at the Stanford 36. Shortly, Mayes ran it in from the 22, capping a wild, five-touchdown bender by the Cougars in 15 minutes, 14 seconds.

Mayes's contribution: touchdown runs of 39, 5, and 22 yards, spliced by the 53-yard screen pass. Oh, yes, he had run 53 yards for a score to give WSU its first touchdown.

Still, in typical WSU fashion, the win wasn't yet sealed. Fred Buckley drove Stanford to the Cougars' 31. On the next play Collins intercepted again at the 11, but trying an ill-advised return, he fumbled the ball at the 18, and Stanford had 58 seconds left to try to tie or win it. "A lot of people have forgotten that," Walden said. "We had to hold 'em again."

They did. Stanford moved to the Cougar 5 with eight seconds left, but the drive expired there after a short pass from Buckley to Brad Muster, and finally it was over. WSU had its best comeback victory in history, 49–42.

Mayes was merely superlative, with 29 carries, 216 rushing yards, and 5 touchdowns. Walden's postgame comments reflected his amazement. "Can you believe this?" he said.

"Frankly, when it was 42–14, I never thought we would win. There just wasn't enough time left. But we try not to get away from the basic stuff, and it paid off."

Recalls Mayes, "It was a real turning point, in terms of enthusiasm in the locker room. There was very much an emotional team celebration in the locker room, singing the Cougar fight song. It just kind of spontaneously came out. Jim [Walden] was in tears."

"Nobody panicked," says Collins. "With the guys you had on offense, you felt you could be in any game."

Another of Mayes's mimeographed quotes after the game turned out both prophetic and ironic. "We finally got the confidence we've been waiting for," he said. "People will see a different Washington State team from now on." In reality, what people saw the next week was more of the same.

The setup for WSU's game at Oregon the next Saturday was unusual. In their annual rivalry fracas with Washington, the Ducks had played the weirdest of games against a team that would go on to win the Orange Bowl and finish second in the country: Oregon allowed the top-ranked Huskies an astonishing three first downs, yet lost 17–10 on defense and special-teams plays.

So Oregon was as ripe as a hothouse tomato for two reasons: Its fever pitch for the Huskies is probably unequaled, and it was coming down from that buzz; and for most of the week, the Duck defenders were applauded on campus and around Eugene for their stout effort at Washington.

Two decades later Mayes remembers the reconnaissance the Cougars did the day before at Oregon's Autzen Stadium. He noticed the field had a distinct "crown," with an appreciable slope. And because of the lay of the AstroTurf nap, the traction was excellent running toward one sideline but treacherous going the other way, where the nap was almost flat. He filed the information away.

At kickoff it was forty-eight degrees, with showers. A modest crowd of 24,874 didn't know that it was about to witness history. Mayes's day began without the promise of anything special. In the first quarter he carried nine times for 41 yards, while the Cougars scored on three of their first four possessions for a 21–6 lead. He was just getting warmed up.

After a punt on the next WSU possession, the Cougars were at their 31 yard line nearing the middle of the second quarter. Out of WSU's veer-option attack, Mayes took a pitch to the right, shed a tackle off his right thigh, burst through a hole, and galloped 69 yards for a touchdown. "That was the one that got me going," he says. "Then we started running the draw—over and over and over."

To hear the Cougars tell it, the draw play became something of an inside joke because of its outrageous success that day. "The center and guard did a cross-block," says Lynch, "and Rueben broke the cut up the middle. If we were able to isolate the middle linebacker, Rueben could sprint into the secondary."

And make no mistake, the Oregon secondary saw a lot of Mayes that day. Starting with that long run with 8:20 left in the half until intermission, Mayes amassed a startling 141 yards on just 7 carries. By halftime, he had 197 yards on 20 carries.

It was all coming within the framework of the game, not for the sake of the numbers. WSU had a 30–20 halftime lead. "The Oregon defensive line and 'backers were quite fast, and their scheme relied upon reading the offensive play and reacting to the flow," said Lynch. "However, our offensive line was built upon attacking the defense and not giving them a chance to react. Therefore, we were able to exploit their strategy as they were sitting back and catching the blocks."

After a penalty on Mayes's first run after halftime, these were his carries in the third quarter: first, 13 yards. Then 7, 16, 5, 11, and 20. It was 37–26, Cougars, heading into the final quarter. On a pitch left, Mayes ran for a 12-yard touchdown early in the fourth quarter. His next two carries were worth 11 and 27 yards. Now he was well beyond the 300-yard mark, closing in on the NCAA record of 356 yards by Eddie Lee Ivery of Georgia Tech against Air Force in 1978.

"By the very end I heard something like, 'Rueben, you're close to some kind of record,'" Mayes says. "I go, 'Really?' It didn't faze me. I was so focused. We were trying to stay in the game."

With 5:23 remaining and WSU ahead 47–41, the Cougars took over at their 34-yard line after Oregon's failed onside kick. Mayes had 327 yards rushing. WSU pieced together three first downs, and finally, on a third-and-eight play at the Oregon 26 with 1:12 left, he carried for 5 yards up the middle—must have been a draw play—and surpassed Ivery by one yard. It set up Traut's field goal, and Washington State won, 50–41, in the highest-scoring game involving Oregon since 1916.

In the *Eugene Register-Guard* the next day, Oregon coach Rich Brooks was quoted, "Mayes is an outstanding running back. He has speed, good moves, and he can run inside or outside. But I thought our defense was non-existent."

Writer John Conrad noted, "Ultimately, the thing to remember about the record is that Mayes set it in a game in which his

Runaway

Twelve times, a back has topped the 1,000-yard mark in a season at Washington State. The man who made it an even dozen did it in an emphatic way and yet an enigmatic one.

In 2005 Jerome Harrison, a 5'10", 200-pound Kalamazoo, Mich. native, weaved for an even 1,900 yards. That shattered a generation-old school record of 1,637 by Rueben Mayes in 1984 and vaulted Harrison to number five on the all-time Pac-10 list past USC's O. J. Simpson (1,880) in his Heisman Trophy–winning year of 1968.

Harrison also proved exceedingly durable. He carried 308 times, far outdistancing the 264 by the previous season leader, Shaumbe Wright-Fair, in 1992. Oddly, Harrison's record burst came in a season in which—largely because of defensive problems—WSU finished only 4–7.

team needed every one of those yards, not some blowout where he was left in to pad his statistics."

The newspaper quoted Rypien as saying, "Every down, every play, every minute, he's giving 100 percent, whether it's in practice or in a game. I feel blessed to be on the same team with him."

It's the stuff of clichés to note that the record wouldn't have happened without the work of the WSU offensive line and blocking by receivers. And as Lynch recalls accurately, "It was with an offensive line that was limited to five players with only one backup. The sixth was even injured so we had to make sure none of us got hurt."

Indeed, the game participation chart backs up Lynch. Only six linemen are listed: Lynch; center Curt Ladines; tackles Mike Dreyer, Jamie White, and Bill Williams; and guard Kirk Samuelson. Collins, the safety, saw a snootful of the 6'0", 208-pound Mayes in practice regularly and fully appreciated him. "He could put a move on you, but that wasn't his deal," Collins says. "He was a bigger guy. He ran with power, and he was tough. Boy, was he smooth, very under control."

Says Walden, "Rueben had an uncanny ability to see the block coming. He could make a cut as he's going through a hole before anybody knew. He had tremendous explosion. His biggest attribute was his speed."

So repetitive was the draw play that Walden remembers a subsequent ribbing from Brooks about it. Quoting the Oregon coach fuming to his staff about it, Walden said, "How can we have every fan in the stadium yelling, 'Watch the draw!' and we can't stop it?"

It wasn't until the next day that Mayes's achievement began to sink in. Publicist Rod Commons summoned him to his office that Sunday morning, telling him there were radio and TV stations lining up to interview him about his 357-yard day. He walked by basketball practice, and heads turned. The basketball team gave him a standing ovation.

Mayes would go on to the NFL and become an all-pro running back. WSU people would say it couldn't have happened to a better guy. But this is also true: There haven't been a whole lot of college running backs better than Rueben Mayes, especially on those two golden Saturdays.

Pasadena Surprise

What if? What if, on the afternoon of October 29, 1988, Washington State hadn't stolen into Rose Bowl Stadium and shocked a top-ranked UCLA team, 34–30? What if there hadn't been a wacked-out hootenanny of crimson and gray on the sidelines that day in Arroyo Seco, with players embracing deliriously and fans ecstatic and the coach's dad, old Pinky Erickson, given the thrill of a lifetime?

It was a day that changed the face of football, not only at Washington State, but college football. "Without a question, it changed my career," says Dennis Erickson, Pinky's son.

It's a safe proposition that, absent his team's stunning upset that day as a 19½-point underdog, Erickson wouldn't have been named coach of the Miami Hurricanes four months later. A career that took him to Miami, then the Seattle Seahawks and San Francisco 49ers, with an interregnum at Oregon State, would somehow have swerved elsewhere.

Without that victory, the Cougars would have dropped to 4–4. They likely would have finished the season maybe 6–5 or 7–4, but probably without a bowl appearance. Without equivocation, we can say they wouldn't have gone 9–3 and given Erickson enough cachet to get the Miami job the next March when Jimmy Johnson was hired by the Dallas Cowboys.

"We had some good athletes, guys that could run, but you've got to win games," Erickson said. "Until you have success doing it, it's just talk. Winning that game was huge in my career, no question."

There were lots of lesser side effects. Around the country, in the offices of people like Timm Rosenbach and Ron Lee and Jim Michalczik, photographed mementoes of that day hang on walls, testament to what was and what can be.

"That's still my favorite game of all time," says Michalczik, an assistant coach at California in the early 2000s. "There's something to a team believing it can win. I still preach that in coaching." Until that day, however, it was a wavering belief. The Cougars had a team that seemed destined to tantalize but not maximize. In the first four weeks of the season, they had scored 137 points to rock three nonleague foes—Illinois, Minnesota, and Tennessee—on the road. But they wrapped that around a home loss to Oregon.

As WSU head coach in 1987–88, Dennis Erickson took the Cougars to a nine-win season with an Aloha Bowl triumph.

In October, they dropped consecutive games to Arizona and Arizona State, falling to 4–3, and looked very much like a team that wouldn't fulfill its promise. Ed Tingstad, a backup running back and now a WSU team physician, recalls Erickson's subdued observation after one of those losses. "Dennis sometimes would just yell," said Tingstad. But on this occasion, Tingstad said, his voice was quiet and even.

Thumbs Up, Mike

The 1991 spinal injury that left Mike Utley paralyzed from the waist down while he was a member of the Detroit Lions shocked and saddened his former teammates. But they came to know him not only as a member of WSU's great 1988 offensive line but as the guy who made the thumbs-up gesture while being taken from the field on that melancholy day.

"You can see him fighting through all the things he's fighting through, and that's why he was a good player," says his WSU coach, Dennis Erickson. "He would have been an all-pro player for a long time."

Utley and his wife live in central Washington, and he attends many WSU home games. He is active in foundation work and the search to find a cure for spinal injuries. "He really just loved life," said former teammate Jim Michalczik. "He'd find a way to make things fun. I don't know if anybody could have overcome and risen above it like Mike has."

Because Utley seemed to love football so much, some worried about him. But his competitive spirit has proven to be indomitable. Ed Tingstad, the WSU team doctor who played with Utley, remembers the night when he felt better about his old teammate. "One night I went shopping," Utley told Tingstad. "I was really depressed. I had just lost girlfriend number 400. I had two bags of groceries and put them on the counter. The bag fell over and a big, one-pound bag of M&M's broke.

"I got out of my chair, got down on my hands and knees, and for the next two hours, picked up every one of those things."

Said Tingstad, "You know, Mike, I think you're going to be OK."

"I think I am, too," said Utley.

Mike Utley was one of the stars of the 1988 offensive line, perhaps the best in school history.

"This is just so disappointing," Erickson said, "because you are so much better than this." He was right. The Cougars had Rosenbach, a future pro, at quarterback. They had an eventual first-round NFL draft pick, running back Steve Broussard. They had an offensive line perhaps unparalleled in school history: tackles John Husby and Chris Dyko, guards Mike Utley and Michalczik and two capable centers, Dave Fakkema and Paul Wulff. "They might have been as good as I've ever been around in college," said Erickson.

It was a team just beginning to taste success. In 1987, Erickson's first season, the Cougars had gone 3–7–1. Rosenbach had thrown 24 interceptions as a sophomore and had actually gone to the coach and suggested he play defensive back.

"He didn't want to play quarterback," Erickson says. "Of course, he didn't have a lot of success that first year. I said, 'You gotta stay, man, you gotta play quarterback.' He had that personality like Brett Favre at that position, a linebacker playing quarterback. He was just tough."

"You wanted to play hard for him," said Michalczik. "Timm wasn't a pretty-boy quarterback." Nor was he resting particularly easy the week leading up to the game. He had thrown an end-zone interception near the end of the ASU game, and WSU's season was slipping away.

After that game, he remembers heading with teammate Jody Sears toward a campus watering hole, where they discovered there was a bomb threat. "It's probably for you," Sears deadpanned.

Rosenbach was also jousting with assistant coach Tim Lappano. While running out of bounds against Arizona State, the nimble Rosenbach had been careless with the ball, bringing an admonition from Lappano. The two had a ritual of warming Rosenbach up before practice, but, remembers Rosenbach, "We didn't talk for like the whole week. My little cocky attitude, I didn't appreciate it [the lecture]. I was under enough stress."

UCLA was led by quarterback Troy Aikman, who was building a good case to win the Heisman Trophy. Aikman would be the number one pick in the 1989 NFL draft. There was tons of talent around him. Three other players—linebacker Carnell Lake, tailback Eric Ball, and cornerback Darryl Henley—were second-round picks in that 1989 draft. The roster was awash in other solid players, among them tight end Charles Arbuckle, nose guard Jim Wahler, linebackers Marvcus Patton and Roman Phifer, and free safety Eric Turner. In retrospect, maybe the Cougars had the Bruins right where they wanted them.

"I remember Coach Erickson saying, 'They don't give you a snowball's chance in hell here,'" said Tingstad. He also recalls the team being almost ignored, before and after the game, by the Los Angeles media. "There was almost this [attitude]: 'You're not supposed to do this to us,'" Tingstad says.

On a hazy, sixty-eight-degree day, a whiff of upset was in the air early for the Cougars. Running back Richie Swinton, filling in for an injured Broussard, gained 7 yards on his first carry. Then Rosenbach hit tight end Doug Wellsandt, Tim Stallworth, and William Pellum for 23, 18, and 11 yards on consecutive plays, and Jason Hanson booted a 48-yard field goal for a 3–0 WSU lead.

The scent of surprise soon disappeared as the Bruins came to control the first half. A couple of field goals by Alfredo Velasco moved UCLA ahead 6–3. In the middle of the second quarter,

Aikman moved the Bruins briskly on a 41-yard drive in six plays for the game's first touchdown.

The Cougars sputtered on their next possession. Aikman marshalled the Bruins 87 yards in nine plays, highlighted by a 33-yard pass to tight end Randy Austin, and UCLA had a 20–3 lead that the Cougars shaved slightly with another Hansen field goal before halftime.

By the break Aikman was 12 of 17 for 150 yards, and the Bruins had possession for more than nineteen minutes. On the other side of the ball, Rosenbach was under a stiff rush. The Cougars had 149 total yards, hardly a yeoman output from one of the school's best offenses in history. Trotting off the field to the locker room, offensive coordinator Bob Bratkowski saw the heavy cables beaming the game on network television. "Cut the cords," he said wryly to Lappano.

As Michalczik remembers it, the offense was appreciative and almost apologetic to the defense at halftime, although the Cougars were hardly stuffing the Bruins. "They'd done a great job of keeping it as close as it was," he said. "For us on offense it was, 'Good job, don't worry, we're going to get straightened out.'" Before it got better, it got worse. The Bruins took the second-half kickoff and blew through the Cougars like a hot Hawaiian wind. It isn't hard to envision UCLA believing this one was in the bag. Aikman moved the Bruins 71 yards in seven plays, none shorter than 4 yards. Ball, who had run for 227 yards in the Rose Bowl as a freshman against Iowa, scored from the 8 and it was 27–6, UCLA.

The Cougars' season was hanging on the precipice. But as Michalczik had promised, the offense began to find itself. Swinton carried the first three times on the ensuing possession for 18 yards. Rosenbach hit Stallworth for 20, and at the UCLA 15, Rosenbach fired a short pass to Stallworth on an option route, and the junior receiver stretched the ball over the goal line to bring WSU within 27–13.

Now the Cougars created a big break on defense. Safety Artie Holmes tagged Ball after a 17-yard run, and he fumbled at the Bruins 37. In five plays, the Cougars moved smartly in, Swinton running over from six yards out to make it 27–20 with fully 6:45 left in the third quarter.

Rosenbach noticed a funny thing happening in that period. "They hadn't been blitzing, they had the game in hand, and they decided to come after us," he said, "probably with the intention of, 'Let's just ice this thing.'"

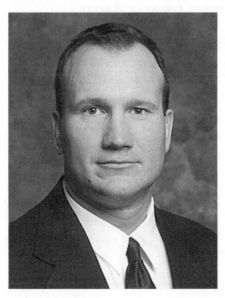

Before he became WSU quarter-backs coach in 2003, Tim Rosenbach starred at the position for the Cougars in 1988.

Booming Booter

Jason Hanson came to Washington State from Spokane's Mead High School without a scholarship. He left with a distinction he still holds: most prolific long-distance kicker in NCAA history.

A soccer, basketball, and football player in high school, Hanson (1988–91) was a walk-on in the regime of head coach Dennis Erickson. He quickly won the placekicking job and had it four years, during which he launched, and made, more long-distance bombs than any kicker.

Entering the 2005 season, Hanson had the NCAA record for 50-yards-or-longer field goals made in a career (20), 40-yarders or longer made (39), and most attempts of 40 or more (66). He also holds the NCAA season record for average distance of field goals made (a staggering 50.9) and attempted (51.2), both in 1991, when he went 10 for 22.

Hanson proved adaptable, too. The NCAA eliminated kicking tees after his freshman year of 1988, and before his senior season, goal posts were narrowed from 23 feet, 4 inches to 18 feet, 6 inches. No matter; Hanson set his school season record of six field goals of 50 yards-plus in 1991.

After graduating from WSU, Hanson went on to a long career with the Detroit Lions.

Seconds remained in the third quarter when the Cougars faced second-and-seven from their 19. Earlier in the game, when WSU had gone to a four-receiver set without a tight end, the Bruins had come with a big blitz, and Rosenbach overthrew Pellum.

"We just said, 'Be ready, if they come up and show that again, this is what we're gonna do,'" Rosenbach said. "We got it again with the 'trips' set, and with Wellsandt at tight end, we had an extra guy in for protection."

Rosenbach retreated three steps, flung a 20-yard strike to Stallworth, and the receiver shed his man-to-man coverage. Stallworth saw nothing but Pasadena green between him and the end zone, and he covered it easily for the touchdown that knotted the game at 27–all.

The crowd numbered 51,970, and it was stunned. Even the smallish size of it—given UCLA's number one status and WSU's entertaining offense—seemed to suggest nobody was expecting a fight on this day.

UCLA struck back with a twelve-play, 60-yard drive for a field goal to take a 30–27 lead. But it was nothing like the march on which the Cougars then embarked. They drove thirteen plays and, officially, ran the ball thirteen plays. Rosenbach tried one pass to Stallworth that fell incomplete, but the Bruins were flagged for defensive holding.

The Cougars were suddenly owners of the line of scrimmage. They ran Swinton no fewer than nine times. Rosenbach, so accustomed to having to be the playmaker, carried the other four. "It was weird for me," Rosenbach says. "It was awesome; it wasn't relying on me." Rosenbach handed off to Swinton at the 1, he pounded it across, and the Cougars had a 34–30 lead with 6:21 remaining.

"You could see in the eyes of their defensive linemen and linebackers," recalls Wulff. "They were basically: 'What's coming next? Is it going to be pass, or play-action, or run?' I remember them not coming off the ball. They got really soft. They didn't know what was hitting them."

The Cougars forced two more turnovers but didn't capitalize. Then they left their supporters with heart palpitations in the final minute. Rob Myers punted to Henley, and he returned it 31 yards to the WSU 39 with less than a minute left. On the first play Arbuckle, the tight end, broke loose over the middle and caught a 33-yard pass from Aikman to the WSU 6. Now WSU's rousing comeback was in peril of being completely forgotten.

Aikman threw for Arbuckle again and then for wideout David Keating, misfiring twice. On third down, he looked for running back Maury Toy over the middle, but Lee, at safety, broke it up. Finally, on fourth down, Aikman flung one toward Keating on an "out" route, but cornerback Vernon Todd had it covered, and the ball fell incomplete. It was over. Referring to the four straight throws, Lee said, "It was surprising they went to the pass. I guess they figured they had Troy Aikman."

Aikman went on to finish third in the Heisman voting. The Cougars, well, they had an irrefutable sign that they were finally arriving. "I really believe it kind of got Washington State going in the right direction," said Erickson.

The coach would leave, and the Cougars would skid again under Mike Price before another revival. But this day, they would hold forever dear in memory and memento. Several of the Cougars have photographs mounted on walls from that game. "I still have the game on 16-millimeter [film]," said Lee, laughing. "It's just hard to find a 16-millimeter projector."

Like some of his old teammates, Lee is now an assistant coach, at Wisconsin. He finds himself drawing on that day in Pasadena, even if it means little to today's players. "It doesn't matter whether they have the ranking, or whatever they are," Lee says. "It's whether you're going to beat the man in front of you."

The man or the monolith. That upset still ranks as the only instance in school history when the Cougars brought to heel a number one team.

Whiteout
Wipeout

You had to be there. You had to be in Pullman the afternoon of November 21, 1992, to understand it. You had to be in attendance at Martin Stadium, in the howling wind and the driving snow and the rollicking good time the Cougars had for three riotous hours against their persistent nemesis, Washington.

To the Huskies, it must have seemed like twenty-three. This was a game that will deepen in the lore of the Apple Cup and become more unthinkable and grow more gilded in the broken annals of WSU victories over Washington.

It need not. On this day, the truth was plenty sufficient; no blandishments necessary. Afterward, WSU's junior linebacker, Anthony McClanahan, called it "The best day of my life." Thousands more would surely call it, at the very least, unforgettable.

On game's eve, there was little buzz that it might snow. The *Moscow-Pullman Daily News* made mention of possible snow "late in the day," but the forecast was paid little heed. Instead, the talk was more about mind-set. The game matched two teams which had been in a lot better shape in late October than they were in late November.

Washington State had finally blossomed in the fourth year of Mike Price's regime. The Cougars had run off six straight victories to begin the season before they were waylaid 31–21 at USC. That began a downward spiral. The next week in Pullman, a favored WSU team fell heavily to Oregon, 34–17. A week later, WSU had to hold off a two-point conversion attempt to thwart Arizona State, 20–18. You couldn't have proven it by the meager 15,441 fans in attendance at Martin Stadium, but with two games left, the Cougars were still in the Rose Bowl race. Ingloriously, WSU plummeted out of it the next week at Stanford, allowing the Cardinal 23 fourth-quarter points in a 40–3 defeat.

Washington's season was more tumultuous. The Huskies had won a share of the 1991 national championship and for much of 1992 seemed bent on repeating. They were unbeaten through October, and then, in the middle of the first week of November, everything changed. The *Seattle Times* broke the story that quarterback Billy Joe Hobert, who had led the team's unbeaten 1991 season, had accepted a $50,000 loan from a benefactor in Idaho, in violation of NCAA rules.

Number one in the country at the time, the Huskies lost their next game at Arizona but clinched a third straight Rose Bowl the next week. They entered the Apple Cup as big, 14-point favorites, but there were two factors arguing otherwise: The motivation of the Rose Bowl was no longer at stake, and the inexorable tentacles of NCAA investigation loomed over them as a result of the Hobert revelation.

The tenor of the day was established when the townsfolk opened their drapes at about 9:00 A.M. Snow was whipping down out of the east. Both teams were headquartered at motels in nearby Moscow. The Cougars, already amped to beat a program which had throttled WSU by a combined 111–31 the previous two years, rocked their team bus at the twin prospects of the snowflakes and the game with their rival. They arrived in Pullman and the snow continued unabated.

"As soon as I saw them [the Huskies] get off the bus to come into the stadium, I knew we had a chance," said WSU coach Mike Price. "They did not want to be in Pullman, and we did."

Mike Pattinson, WSU's backup quarterback to Drew Bledsoe, remembers emerging from the tunnel for pregame warm-ups and feeling dread. Then he looked at Bledsoe's face, "and it was almost just a look of glee." Pattinson had grown up in Moscow and never played in snow. In fact, while the urban myth is that the Cougars were accustomed to the white stuff, that wasn't true. They hadn't been to a bowl game since 1988 and thus hadn't had any late practices in snow.

"I remember warming up with him," Pattinson said, referring to Bledsoe. "Here I am throwing this ball capable of breaking knuckles, and Drew's throwing a perfect spiral."

Carousel Behind Center

Perhaps no school in history became as enmeshed in a quarterback controversy as deep as the Cougars did in 1990, particularly when they traveled to USC. WSU didn't have two quarterbacks involved; it had three. And they had all been recruited by different coaching staffs.

Brad Gossen was a holdover from the Jim Walden regime that ended in 1986. Aaron Garcia had been signed by Dennis Erickson's staff. And there was a tall gunslinger who became head coach Mike Price's signature recruit, a fellow named Drew Bledsoe, who was a true freshman in 1990.

The Cougars were 2–3 headed to USC, and Price essentially put the job up for grabs. Gossen started, but with WSU behind 14–0 with more than five minutes left in the first quarter, Garcia relieved him. Garcia had the reins until halftime. Bledsoe took the first series of the third quarter, but Gossen reappeared midway through the quarter. He stayed at the controls until early in the fourth quarter, when Bledsoe came back.

USC won, 30–17. The final numbers: Gossen, 7 for 13 for 86 yards; Garcia, 6 for 13 for 63 yards and two interceptions; and Bledsoe, 6 for 12 for 145 yards and a touchdown. "There was a lot of division," Price said fifteen years later, referring to team chemistry. "I couldn't get everybody together. If I'd gone with Gossen, there were two factions that didn't like it. If I'd gone with Garcia, then the Gossen and Bledsoe guys wouldn't have liked it."

So he went with sheer talent and his own guy. The next game, Bledsoe made his first start, and he had the job for the rest of his two and a half seasons at Washington State.

Depending on whether your persuasion is Cougar crimson and gray or Washington purple and gold, the game might already have been won before the 12:30 P.M. kickoff on ABC. In 2002, the respective equipment managers who were on the two sides ten years earlier told the *Seattle Times* that there was a difference in the style of shoes worn that day. Wendell Neal, WSU's equipment manager, said the Cougars took the field for pregame warm-ups in regular artificial-turf shoes. Pattinson recalls those as being a relatively flat-bottomed shoe that players usually favored on a fast track because it didn't grab as much and thus put knees and ankles at risk. But on this day, something different was in order. "We came in and changed forty-some pairs of shoes," Neal told the newspaper. "We had considerably better footing. Obviously, it's still slippery, but it was like they [the Huskies] were on roller skates."

Said Pattinson, "I remember a lot of guys changing to the mock cleat, just a very small, maybe quarter-inch cleat, a more grippy turf shoe. That really seemed to make a difference for us."

Tony Piro, Washington's equipment manager, confirmed Neal's account, saying that the Huskies had tested the Nike "Destroyer" model shoe known for its traction but had switched back to a different Converse model.

As kickoff neared, a snowplow scraped sidelines and yard lines. But within minutes, the markers were covered by what would become a several-inch snowfall. It's hard to know whether Torey Hunter's observation is retrospective bravado or heartfelt sentiment, but the standout WSU cornerback says today he was disappointed to see the snow. "We didn't want any excuses," he said. "I just remember knowing it was going to be ugly for them."

Game-time temperature was thirty-two degrees. At 2:00 P.M., the wind was measured at 22 miles per hour. Many longtime observers of the Apple Cup consider it the worst conditions for the game in history. There was thus a suspicion among many that as the game began, it might take only a single score to win it. How faulty that notion would be.

The Cougars took the opening kickoff and moved quickly for a touchdown, driving 80 yards into the storm in nine plays. But the conversion attempt hit the upright. The Huskies responded with a 40-yard drive early in the second quarter. When they succeeded on the PAT, they took a 7–6 halftime lead that seemed larger than the single point.

Washington State obliterated that single-point deficit with a quarter the likes of which it has never seen. The histrionics began with 11:36 left in the third quarter, on the play of the day and certainly in the top ten of any living Cougar. At the Washington 44 yard line, Bledsoe dropped back and lofted a pass deep toward the back of the west end zone.

Mike Levenseller, the WSU offensive coordinator who was in his first season of coaching with the Cougars, says receiver Phillip Bobo was "supposed to run a streak." When Bledsoe saw a UW safety "bite" on the run, Bledsoe threw for C. J. Davis, who was running a post route with a touchdown in mind. Somehow, Bobo got involved. He and Davis converged on the ball simultaneously, just as they confronted a snowbank. Video replays show Davis leaping for the ball, coming down in disappointment without it, and discovering, to his delight, that it was Bobo who had snatched it away.

Even in the waning years of a sterling NFL career, Drew Bledsoe called the 1992 Apple Cup in the snow his most enjoyable game.

Fields's Hard Road

Mark Fields was one of the best linebackers in the history of Washington State. A 6'2", 240-pound hunk of granite from Cerritos, California, he played for the 1992 and 1994 WSU teams, each of which won bowls. In 1994, he was a member of one of the Cougars' all-time best defenses, winning third-team AP All-America honors.

A first-round draft pick by the New Orleans Saints, Fields has known his share of postcollegiate hardship. As a member of the Carolina Panthers, he was diagnosed with Hodgkin's Disease in August 2003 and sat out that season while undergoing chemotherapy and radiation treatments. He made a triumphant return in 2004 and even was selected to the Pro Bowl for the second time in his career. But a recurrence of the condition was discovered again in the spring of 2005, and at thirty-two, he sat out that fall while undergoing further treatment.

Bledsoe bounced on the balls of his feet as he awaited the catch, then sprinted toward the end zone. And you understood how, deep into a professional career that saw him drafted number one and play in a Super Bowl, he would call that Apple Cup the "most favorite game I've played in." Then the points came easily and often. Midway through the quarter, Bledsoe bought time and rifled a 15-yard touchdown pass to Calvin Schexnayder.

It was time for the running game to take over. Less than three minutes later, senior back Shaumbe Wright-Fair blew 51 yards on a quick-hitter to make it 28–7 and the rout was on. Wright-Fair later would add a 41-yard run for a score on a day on which he rushed for 194 yards, at that time tying him for number seven on the school list. WSU capped its madcap third quarter when offensive lineman Konrad Pimiskern recovered a fumble in the end zone. That made it a 29-point period, and WSU eventually put the wraps on a 42–23 victory.

"We were pretty good at throwing the ball," said Levenseller. "I don't care what the weather was. They were going to cheat those safeties down and we were going to throw the ball regardless. And Shaumbe was a hell of a back." Bledsoe completed 18 of 30 passes for 260 yards and 2 touchdowns, with one interception. It was one of the extraordinary individual performances in the history of the Apple Cup series.

After WSU players had shed their football gear, Bledsoe accompanied Price to Hollingbery Fieldhouse, where a crowd of exuberant Cougar faithful greeted them, chanting "One more year!" to the WSU quarterback. Alas, their advice went unheeded; Bledsoe entered the draft the next spring and became the number one pick of the New England Patriots.

Meanwhile, the Huskies couldn't catch a break even after time expired. Bruce King, a television sportscaster in Seattle, carried through with plans to do his postgame show from high above Martin Stadium, on the balcony of the Compton Union Building. The perch made for the proper background, but it must have been added torture for UW defensive coordinator Jim Lambright, fielding questions alongside King and WSU assistant coach Ted Williams.

About then, something totally bizarre was happening. The snow was disappearing, giving way to warmer chinook winds and rain. People who had spent halftime on the phone trying to secure motel rooms found the roads out of town open and friendly. It was as though the Cougars had ordered up a snowstorm to span the game, and when they had finished their bacchanal, some crimson and gray spirit had raised a hand and advised the gods, "That's enough."

That sort of serendipity surrounded the day for WSU. It couldn't have had a better trigger man than the rangy Bledsoe at quarterback; he has huge hands, and if the ball ever slipped from them, nobody in the crowd of 37,600 noticed. "It was just shocking for me to sit on the sideline and watch the calm manner in which Drew played that game," said Pattinson. "I had a party that night at my house. Drew came over and [tight end] Brett Carolan. I didn't play that game; I sat back and listened. They just talked about it like it was the greatest experience they ever had."

The reach of that game has proved considerable. It has given way to the notion that every time the Apple Cup is in Pullman, there is a distinct threat of snow. Never mind that a spokesman for the National Weather Service said in 2002 that the chance of

2 inches or more of snow on November 21 in Pullman is only 6 percent. All that matters is that that day, the Cougars' number came up, although they will dispute until closing time whether they really needed it.

"Who knows what would have happened?" Levenseller asked rhetorically, referring to a dry afternoon that never materialized. "We don't have to know."

From Rags to Roses

No wonder it took sixty-seven years. No wonder Cougar fans suffered for generations, never tasting the sweet nectar of a Rose Bowl appearance from 1930 to 1997. If it took the exotic mix of the 1997 team to get to Pasadena, all its disparate parts and loopy subplots, maybe it's not a surprise that legions of WSU faithful grew to believe that going to the Rose Bowl was a province of those at USC and Washington and UCLA but not at Washington State.

This was a harmonic convergence, a confluence of divine circumstance climaxed in the late afternoon of November 22, 1997, by a light rain at Husky Stadium. The moment so enraptured Shawn McWashington, one of the WSU receivers, that he waxed poetic: "It was tears," McWashington observed, "from Babe Hollingbery."

Even the Babe himself, probably the best coach in school history, might not have believed the Cougars were ever going to see the Rose Bowl again. They had come close in the war years of 1941–42 under Hollingbery. A loss to California denied them in 1958. The "Cardiac Kids" of 1965 had threatened but come up shy. Jim Walden's 1981 team had taken it down to the Apple Cup but was turned back by the Huskies. Mike Price's 1994 team had the defense but far too little offense. And then came 1997, eclectic and electric.

The quarterback, of course, was Ryan Leaf, who had such an imposing arm and vision that he was the number two pick in the NFL draft of 1998. But McWashington insists that in the spring of 1997, it was Steve Birnbaum, not Leaf, who was "drafted" as the number one quarterback for the spring game by the seniors.

Surely no WSU quarterback has had such an accomplished group of receivers, who dubbed themselves the Fab Five: McWashington, Chris Jackson, Shawn Tims, Kevin McKenzie, and Nian Taylor. They were such characters—sometimes even during games—that McWashington claims that, as a prank, two of them called a security guard at Oregon's Autzen Stadium because a front-row fan was shooting spitballs at them, and when the cops discovered the fan had two outstanding warrants, they hauled him off to jail.

Mike Price was known as a strong motivator and a player's coach.

The running back was Michael Black, who had done time at sixteen in Los Angeles for auto theft and armed robbery. Up front, there was an offensive line dotted with guys who kept achieving beyond expectation, people like center Lee Harrison, who carried a high grade-point average in civil engineering. It was also a group with two starters who had worked through the tragic dynamic of a fatal auto accident a year before.

The defense was less decorated but at least complementary. At tackle was the late Leon Bender, who would die of a seizure before a promising career could begin with the Oakland Raiders. His last act of the 1996 season was to incur disciplinary action from his coaches for chasing an official to the locker room.

End Dorian Boose had signed with the Cougars out of high school and then, as Price says, "took the long way around," going to junior college, getting married, redshirting at WSU before finally producing.

There was linebacker Steve Gleason, at 5'11" too small to play his position, except Bill Doba, the defensive coordinator, had a thing about small, quick 'backers. Gleason was all set to go to Stanford under Bill Walsh, and then one day Walsh was gone and Tyrone Willingham took over, and, says Gleason, "His words basically were, 'You don't have the toughness to play in the Pac-10.'"

Many of the Cougars say they could see something good developing for 1997, but if they did, it was a phenomenon slow to declare itself. The 1996 team had finished 5–6 with four straight losses, the last in overtime to Washington. "You kind of saw flashes there," McWashington says. "That was the first time where Leaf really started to distribute the ball to a lot of people."

In the off-season, WSU athletic director Rick Dickson made a bold scheduling move. In order to get on ABC television, the Cougars agreed to a switch of a November game with UCLA to an August 31 opening. It was enticing for the Bruins because it removed the prospect of a cold, inclement Saturday in Pullman.

For the Cougars it meant a rare, treacherous season debut against UCLA and USC.

"One of the things we did well was, we said, 'This is a great opportunity,'" Price recalls. "It wasn't like, 'How could Dickson have done this?'"

In fall camp, there were positive signs. McWashington remembers one day when Leaf faded to throw an "out" route, Boose rushed madly from the edge and intercepted at almost point-blank range. "Boose and Bender," McWashington says, "you saw them make that type of play constantly."

Gleason remembers a night when Mike Levenseller, the team's wide receivers coach, got up and addressed the team. All the groundwork had been laid, he said, all the multiple pieces necessary were now in place. "This," Levenseller said, "is the team I've been waiting for, guys."

A year earlier, the Cougars had endured tragedy. On July 14, 1996, guard Jason McEndoo and tackle Ryan McShane were returning to Pullman from guard Cory Withrow's wedding in Auburn on the west side of the state with McEndoo's wife of one month, Michelle. While driving, McShane fell asleep momentarily on Interstate 90 near the town of Ellensburg. As he overcorrected, the Ford Explorer rolled several times, ejecting Michelle, who was sleeping in the back seat. She was killed; the two players suffered only minor injuries.

Back in Auburn that day, Withrow and his new wife Kiersten were opening gifts at her parents' home when the phone rang, informing them there had been an accident. A couple of hours before, Michelle McEndoo had sung in their wedding.

"My whole insides just kind of jumped out," Withrow says.

They piled into a car and drove toward Ellensburg. At the hospital they found McEndoo and McShane, holding hands, blind with grief, "one of the toughest things I've ever witnessed in my life," Withrow says.

McEndoo urged the newlyweds to follow through on their honeymoon to Jamaica. They did but were so distracted they came home two days early.

In the succeeding weeks McEndoo was torn. Could he forgive the teammate who had been his best friend? "The '96 season was obviously a very difficult one," he says. "I was just getting by."

First, he had had to make the decision whether to play. He concluded he would be too lost without it. He was spending hours with the team's sports psychologist. Finally one day McEndoo remembers, "I just said, 'I forgive him.' I kind of went back and forth, like anybody would. I had to move on." So they did, and now it was thirteen months removed from the tragedy.

August 31, 1997, was a hot day in Pullman. Nobody knew it at the time, but it matched two teams that would combine for only three regular-season losses.

UCLA took the opening kickoff, and WSU took the field without Bender, who would be its only first-team all-league defender in 1997. The big tackle had been disciplined by Price for something that happened nine months earlier. In Washington's 31–24 Apple Cup victory, the Huskies scored first in overtime, and WSU looked to answer. On the Cougars' second play of the extra period at the UW 7, Black bolted to the Washington 1, but WSU was flagged for holding, setting it back to the 21 yard line. A tying, fourth-down pass was ruled out of bounds and the Huskies survived.

Jason McEndoo overcame the death of his wife to become a key player on the 1997 Rose Bowl team.

"We didn't think it had anything to do with the play," Doba said, recalling the flag. "It was a guy in the backfield that pushed late. Anyway, [Bender] chased that official down the tunnel, he was going to go after him, so Mike made him write a letter of apology to that official and said he wasn't going to start the UCLA game."

On UCLA's second play from scrimmage, the Bruins' stand-out back, Skip Hicks, blew through the very spot where Bender would have been for a 92-yard run and scored two plays later with only sixty-three seconds elapsed. Doba looked at Price, who barked, "That's long enough. Get him in there!"

"That was Leon's suspension," Doba laughed, "for about two plays."

Down 14–3 in the second quarter, the Cougars exploded for 27 unanswered points to take a 30–14 halftime lead. Black, who had 27 carries for 102 yards, scored on a 17-yard run, and Taylor gave the Cougars the lead for good on a 57-yard scoring pass from Leaf. Taylor was eating the Bruins alive; he finished with an even 200 yards on 5 catches.

It would, however, be a bittersweet day for Taylor, who sprained an ankle in the second half. Jackson replaced him in the lineup, turned a short route into a 78-yard touchdown in the third quarter, and ended up as WSU's receiving-yardage leader with 1,005 for the season.

While the Cougars munched up 529 yards of total offense against the Bruins, there were some severely nervous moments down the stretch. Remember, this was a UCLA team that later put up 66 points on both Texas and Houston and would win the Cotton Bowl over Texas A&M.

WSU led most of the fourth quarter, 37–34. Then UCLA drove to the Cougar 1-yard line and inside the three-minute mark, faced a fourth-and-one situation. Hicks had 27 carries for 190 yards to that point.

Then a strange thing happened. Hicks asked out of the game, later claiming he was physically exhausted, and was replaced by a much smaller back, freshman Jermaine Lewis. Afterward, UCLA coach Bob Toledo would be second-guessed for not calling time-out to allow Hicks to gather himself.

Meanwhile, something almost as odd was happening on the other side of the ball. "The strength of the formation was to their left, our right," Doba recalls. "I can't remember who the safety was, but he lined up on the wrong side. They're running a play to their left, right where we didn't have anybody."

Frantically, Doba tried to call timeout on the sideline, but his plea went unheeded. Lewis pounded the ball into the line and was met—as fate would have it—by Bender, who dropped him at the 1. "Had he bounced outside," said Doba, "I think he could have walked in."

It was still dicey. McWashington says he talked Price into a different route after seeing that a UCLA cornerback was turning and running rather than playing "press" coverage, and he caught a first-down pass near the sideline. When McWashington caught another Leaf throw on a post route, the Cougars were able to run out the clock. "When we beat UCLA, I don't think we realized how good that team was," says Gleason.

There was not the vaguest possibility of overconfidence on WSU's part. USC was WSU's forever nemesis, having beaten the Cougars nine straight times and fifteen straight at the Los Angeles Coliseum dating back to 1957. Then there was this: If the Cougars could manage to knock off the 7-point-favorite Trojans, they would become the first team in college history to open a season with victories over the two LA powers. It was hardly a vintage USC team, one that would finish 6–5. But the Trojans were a very large skeleton in the Cougars' closet.

Washington State got out quickly on touchdowns by McWashington and Black and had the game seemingly in hand, 21–6, at halftime. But among WSU traditions, this one is prominent: Things will never be as easy as they might seem.

R. Jay Soward returned the second-half kickoff 95 yards for a touchdown, and another Trojan score, followed by a two-point conversion, knotted the game at 21 early in the fourth quarter.

The teams traded possessions, and with WSU having gone scoreless for twenty-five minutes on the game clock, the Cougars finally struck. Leaf, on third-and-12, threw to McKenzie for 31 yards to the WSU 49, setting up the climactic play.

McWashington recalls a run being called in the huddle. Jackson was split left, Tims to the right, and McWashington and McKenzie were inside Tims. McWashington says in all his study of WSU video and games during and since, he hasn't seen the ball thrown to the inside receiver in that situation. But as the slot receivers signaled the audible to the outside, Tims was late getting the call and tardy off the line, eliminating that option.

Leaf thus unloaded the ball to McKenzie, who snagged it with one hand. Now USC defensive back Antuan Simmons converged on McKenzie, who was being accompanied by McWashington.

It hadn't begun as a banner day for McWashington. On an early screen pass to Black, he missed a block that might have sprung him for a touchdown. A few plays later, he ran a bad pattern and USC's Brian Kelly intercepted. McWashington had come to the sideline, and "Coach Levy [Mike Levenseller] just rips me about those two plays. Just undressed me on the phone."

Now McWashington's moment was at hand. All of it welled up, everything, the forty years of drought in Los Angeles against USC, the whole works. "It was like SC, the biggest stage, ABC," McWashington says. "I took all that and basically put it underneath Antuan Simmons' chin." McEndoo called it an "unbelievable" block. McWashington says, "You could hear the collective gasp from the crowd."

Signal Call

In its August 31, 1998, football issue, *Sports Illustrated* magazine assembled a mythical "Perfect Team," combining the top positional legacies of some NCAA schools to come up with a dream unit.

For the quarterback spot *SI* chose Washington State, which to that point had produced Jack Thompson, Mark Rypien, Timm Rosenbach, Drew Bledsoe, and Ryan Leaf. Later, it would add Jason Gesser.

Wrote *SI*: "Combine a pro-style passing game with a coach, Mike Price, who loves to teach it and free-spirited quarterbacks, and you get an explosive offense. You also get two quarterbacks (Bledsoe and Leaf) taken among the first two picks in the NFL draft over the past decade, a legacy unmatched by any other program over that span."

The rest of the way to the end zone was an easy journey for McKenzie, who finished a 107-yard day as the Cougars won 28–21. Leaf had followed his 381-yard afternoon against UCLA with a 355-yard effort versus USC.

"That's one game I'll never forget," Doba says. "I always talk about, 'Stop and smell the roses.' Judy [his wife] and I walked down the tunnel and back down to the field. The band and the [Trojan] horse were coming up the tunnel the other way. We walked out and took a good look around to just enjoy the moment."

No doubt, it was an occasion to savor. It wouldn't be WSU's last one that season.

■ ■ ■

Now, with a 2–0 record starting the strange, front-loaded 1997 schedule, the Cougars faced some soft spots. So they thought, anyway. First, they had a televised game at lowly Illinois. Kickoff was at 9:30 A.M. Pacific time, and that, combined with the rush of the previous two games, made for a perfect spot for a letdown.

So, it turned out, did the start of the game. On the Cougars' first play from scrimmage, Leaf dumped a 5-yard slant to McKenzie, and he took it the distance for an 80-yard touchdown. Sixteen seconds in, WSU led 7–0.

Then, as McWashington describes it, "We just put it on cruise control." To a fault, almost. Illinois hung in and even had the lead late in the third quarter before Leaf threw for three more touchdowns and DeJuan Gilmore scored on a 21-yard run. WSU survived, 35–22.

The next week's polls found the Cougars number fifteen entering a game in Pullman with Boise State—before Boise State was Boise State. There wouldn't have been much buildup, except for a verbal salvo from BSU kicker Todd Belcastro, a graduate of Mead High in Spokane. Belcastro was quoted in a Boise newspaper as being upset that he wasn't recruited by WSU, making inflammatory comments about the game.

Alas, Belcastro never got much of a chance to showcase his talent. The Cougar defense held Boise State to 115 total yards, WSU rolled up 565, and it was Washington State kicker Rian Lindell who booted a 57-yard field goal in a 58–0 win.

Shawn McWashington, one of the Fab Five receivers, wanted to know the big picture on offensive plays, not just route-running.

Levenseller calls McWashington "probably the smartest receiver I've ever coached. He even wanted to know protections, what the running back and guard were doing." McKenzie was "very quick, a big-play guy, probably best at making the hot read and making the 4-yard catch go to the end zone."

"Tims," says Levenseller, "to this day is the quickest player I've coached and the strongest. He still holds the squat record for receivers here." Jackson "might have been the most complete guy I've ever had. He had a great ability to run great routes. And he could just plant on a dime."

And then there was Taylor, whose 22 catches were least among the five. But his average per catch was a ridiculous 25.9

Mike Levenseller brings a passion for the game to his position group, the wide receivers.

yards. "I'd walk into a meeting on the first day of the week," Levenseller says, "and they'd already have their ideas on the board, what they thought they could do."

It must have been the most unlikely convergence of good receivers in history. McKenzie was a high school running back in Long Beach, California. McWashington was a quarterback in Seattle. Tims was a walk-on from Vallejo, California, who came to WSU with the idea of playing baseball. Taylor spent his last two years of high school in Riverside, California, as a running back. And Jackson had transferred from Cal-Riverside, where he had played point guard in basketball. The school had no football team.

With a 4–0 start, the Cougars returned to Pac-10 play and muscled past Oregon in Eugene, 24–13. The Ducks had a 415–351 edge in total offense, but WSU got interceptions from cornerback Dee Moronkola, defensive tackle Gary Holmes, and safety Duane Stewart.

Soon, the receivers had their alter ego in the offensive line, self-dubbed the "Fat Five." Some of its parts, too, were improbable. Harrison, a product of Bend, Oregon, was a member of National Honor Society in high school and a walk-on at WSU. "I tried to get Harrison to transfer to Division III schools," Price says. "He wouldn't do it. Lee Harrison was never good enough, until he got a chance to play."

It was something similar with Withrow, albeit on a higher level. Says Price, "I sat Cory Withrow down at the Rose Bowl and said, 'You're too small. You're not good enough. You've got a great wife. Be a high school football coach in Spokane.'" With that advice, Withrow became a longtime lineman with the Minnesota Vikings.

Meanwhile, McEndoo's jagged world had smoothed somewhat. "I was visiting the Sports Page a little bit," he said, referring to a popular local hangout. "She was a bartender. It was like God had delivered an angel." Her name was Ruth, and they had a class together. Later, they would marry and have children, and he would go on to coach at Montana State.

It was something McEndoo noticed in film study the week before the Cal game that helped toward a wild 63–37 WSU victory. When one side of the defensive line did a "twist," the other side did the exact opposite move. "They did it 100 percent," McEndoo says. "You almost didn't believe it."

He took the piece of reconnaissance to the coaches, and they worked out a "pretty complicated" system of audibles and line calls. What followed was an unanswered 42-point first-half explosion that inundated the Bears, and the Cougars finished with 619 yards on only sixty-five plays.

It was in that game that McEndoo learned the reach of Leaf's ability. The defense had just created a turnover in the first half, and in the huddle, according to McEndoo, Leaf said, "All right, guys, give me time on this one, and it'll be a touchdown." "It was like something out of a movie," McEndoo says. "He said it with kind of that gunslinger swagger."

It went for a touchdown. And he did it again in the second half. "Defenses had to make a decision whether they wanted to stop the run or the pass," McEndoo says. "If you wanted to stop Michael Black, you'd put six guys in the box. If they wanted to stop Leaf, they'd put five. If they wanted to stop the pass, Black had big rushing days. If they wanted to stop the run, Ryan had big passing days."

Sometimes it seemed easy for the offense, but the next two games were anything but. Despite a 3–4 record, Arizona came to Pullman bent on an upset, taking a 14–0 first-quarter lead behind gifted freshman quarterback Ortege Jenkins.

The Cougars played catchup most of the game. It was 28–all going into overtime, and it took WSU nine plays to stick the ball into the end zone on Leaf's 1-yard sneak.

Ryan Leaf's 3,968 yards passing in the Rose Bowl season of 1997 is easily the best ever at WSU.

Arizona came right back to score and decided to go for broke, eschewing the conversion kick for a two-point try to win the game and put the first blemish on WSU's season. "Jenkins rolls out and the safety runs in support," Doba recalls. "And the back-side tight end releases. There isn't anybody within 15 yards of this guy. Jenkins could have thrown it over backwards, but he didn't see the guy. He tucks that thing and tries to run."

He was met at the 2 by Stewart and cornerback LeJuan Gibbons. Jenkins tried to fumble into the end zone, but Holmes came up with the ball, and by a 35–34 final, WSU was still unscathed. Most of the season's headlines were grabbed by the offense, but this was a day for the defense to exult. The 34 points notwithstanding, it had held the Wildcats to 319 yards and made the telling play. "Wow," says Gleason, "that was magical."

Tenth-ranked now, the Cougars were 7–0 and had everybody's attention. They were headed into November, to Arizona State (5–2) and a sellout of 73,644. For most of the first half, WSU played miserably, falling behind 24–0.

McWashington remembers ASU safety Mitchell "Fright Night" Freedman setting the early tone against Black. "Fright Night comes out of nowhere and just levels him," McWashington says. "From that point on, Michael Black gets the ball, he's looking for Fright Night."

But the Cougars were too good offensively to go so quietly. Leaf distributed the ball, the defense stiffened, and McWashington had the game of his life: 5 catches for 162 yards. And when Leaf rushed over a two-point conversion early in the fourth quarter, the Cougars had strung together 25 straight points for a 25–24 lead.

Leaf, Before the Fall

Ryan Leaf went from college hero to professional bust, leading WSU to the 1997 Rose Bowl before a pro career that flamed out spectacularly. His coaches remember him a lot more fondly than will NFL historians.

Then-defensive coordinator Bill Doba recalls how, in the last padded practice of 1994, when Leaf was a scout-team quarterback, WSU's great defense picked him up on its shoulders and carried him off the field. It had appreciated Leaf's brazen, sometimes bawdy attitude, when he would actually insert his own verbal potshots toward defenders into his cadence at the line, as in "blue 14, Jones is a wimp, X-42 . . ." or "Tag 7, red 42, Smith needs a haircut . . ."

He didn't care. Once, secondary coach Craig Bray badgered him about "looking off" receivers when the quarterback he was supposed to be impersonating stared them down. "There, how's that?" Leaf said brashly, doing a grossly exaggerated stare at a receiver, and Bray leaped into his face.

In 1997, a tradition developed. Every Thursday night, as Leaf and the other quarterbacks watched videotape, Joyce Price, the head coach's wife, would bring them a homemade pumpkin pie, Leaf's favorite.

As the Rose Bowl drew near, Leaf inquired about the possibility of a pie, and Mike Price, feigning annoyance, brushed it off. Then on game's eve, there was a knock on Leaf's door: It was Joyce Price, holding a pumpkin pie. "He burst into tears and said, 'I love you guys so much. I knew you wouldn't let me down,'" Mike Price says. "That's the Ryan Leaf I remember."

ASU returned serve for a touchdown, and then WSU would be done in by turnovers. Marching to the ASU 23, the Cougars had a fourth-and-three when Freedman blitzed through the middle of the WSU line and collisioned Leaf, who fumbled, and lineman Hamilton Mee took it 69 yards for the clinching score with 2:55 left. The Sun Devils prevailed, 44–31.

After the ASU loss, the Cougars fell to sixteenth the next week, and indeed, out of the national-title picture. Still, the Rose Bowl was hardly a trifling goal for WSU.

So dominant were the Cougars the next week in a 77–7 victory over Southwestern Louisiana that they held a 42–0 lead before the Ragin' Cajuns mustered a first down. A week later, WSU was less than overwhelming, bedeviled by three touchdowns by Stanford's Troy Walters, but came back for a 38–28 win.

Now the prize was right in front of the Cougars. True, they needed a little help; because of tiebreaking considerations, they had to win and either have UCLA beat USC—the Bruins were tied with the Cougars at the top of the Pac-10—or have Arizona upset Arizona State six days later.

They would have to do it in Seattle, where WSU hadn't won since 1985 with Mark Rypien at quarterback. Even at that, and with the fact the 7–3 Huskies were richly talented—the preseason number one pick by the *New York Times*—it was odd that WSU was a 6-point underdog.

Sunday, with the anticipation already crackling, Price addressed the team, warning it about firing any verbal volleys toward the archrival Huskies. The message took so well that Price awoke the next morning to see a flaming headline in the *Spokane Spokesman-Review* and these quotes from Chris Jackson: "I just

Chris Jackson made some bold comments before the 1997 Apple Cup, then backed them up with some superlative play.

want to go in there, study film on them, and go do what we set out to do, go in and kill them," Jackson was quoted. He went on to say that lesser offenses than the Cougars had put up 40 points on the Huskies, "so we're looking forward to studying them pretty well and going out to put 40, 50 points on them." And this zinger: "I'll be damned if I'm going to let the Huskies get in my way of going to the Rose Bowl."

At 7:00 A.M., Price could hardly summon Jackson to his office fast enough. He slammed his hand on his desk. "I was so mad, just furious at him," Price says. "I said, 'There's no back door to get out of now. If you don't do this, you're the dumb one.'"

Says Jackson, "I just spoke very confidently about our team. I don't think I knocked them in any way. I didn't mean it to come across as cocky, but we were confident."

At the team hotel in Lynnwood the night before the game, the seniors staged skits. It was Jackson who did an impersonation of Price, finally cracking a weeklong burn inside the head coach. And then Jackson went out and had the game of his life.

It was a day to sell out. Gleason, a callow, 215-pound sophomore who began the season thinking that "more than anything, I need not to be the weak link on this squad," took on Washington's 280-pound tight end, Cam Cleeland, in a futile attempt at a shoulder-high tackle. Gleason got up with sirens going off in his head and staggered off, but his teammates rallied around that kind of effort.

The Huskies scored first, but the Cougars put together a solid second quarter, punctuated by one of the plays of the day. With the game tied at 7, Leaf saw "press" coverage by UW cornerback Mel Miller on Jackson and audibled to a "go" route. Jackson beat Miller, made the catch, and saw Husky safety Tony Parrish pounding toward him. Parrish, a future pro, had an upper body seemingly chipped from granite. "He put his head down, and I put my head down," said Jackson. "He fell backwards. I remember pulling my shoe from him."

Jackson finished a 57-yard scoring play, and the Cougars would never trail again. They led 17–7 at half. "You could just see the look in their face," says McWashington, recalling Jackson's shedding of Parrish. "Like, 'That doesn't happen. Who does that?'"

But the Huskies wouldn't go away, even after WSU lineman Rob Rainville fell on a Black fumble in the end zone to open the scoring in the second half, putting WSU up, 24–7. Washington countered with two touchdowns in three minutes, one on an interception return by Parrish, before Jackson struck again late in the third period. He took a pass from Leaf and outraced Parrish down the sideline for a 50-yard score, making it 31–21, WSU.

Every time the Cougars took a double-digit lead, the Huskies clawed back. With nine seconds left, Brock Huard threw to Jerome Pathon to make it 41–35, WSU, and Washington lined up for an onside kick. After sixty-seven years of exasperation, it was still possible for the Huskies to recover and drive a stake into Washington State hearts with a miracle play.

Not. The Cougars fell on the kick, and the party began. UCLA had beaten USC, 31–24, and finally, pigs flew. Washington State was headed to the Rose Bowl.

Players were lifted onto shoulders. WSU fans mounted the goal posts, joined by a reserve defensive back, Kenny Moore. Price sought out Jackson, who had 8 catches for 185 yards, grabbed him, and shouted, "From here on out, you can make any prediction you want to!"

Leaf had 358 yards passing on 22 of 38, Black had 37 carries for 170 yards, but the defense contributed in a huge way, as a key mid-season personnel move came home to roost. The Cougars shifted Chris Jackson's brother Ray from safety to corner to shore up a weakness there and plugged freshman Lamont Thompson into Ray Jackson's safety spot. Against the Huskies, Thompson contributed 3 of WSU's 5 interceptions and had a team-high 12 tackles.

That night the coaches partied at their hotel. Chris Jackson and his fiancée hung out with Leaf's family. Gleason, a Spokane product, sought out old high school friends going to Washington, stayed the night with them, and found them, "like, pumped for me. We ended up having a great time. It was fun to cruise around campus and go, 'Hey, man, we're going to the Rose Bowl'—to know that this is as good as it gets."

For legions of WSU faithful, that described it. They floated for weeks, experiencing something many had assumed they would never know. Tickets for the Rose Bowl against Michigan were at a premium, scalped for as much as $900, and there were lofty estimates that WSU could have sold 300,000 tickets.

In Pasadena, the Cougars struck first on Leaf's 15-yard touchdown pass to McKenzie late in the first quarter. But Heisman Trophy winner Charles Woodson made a pivotal play moments later, intercepting Leaf in the end zone as he threw for McKenzie on a corner route.

"It wasn't the Cougar Leaf," McWashington joked, referring to the interception. "It was the San Diego Charger Leaf. If we go up 14 points, Michigan's not coming back."

The undefeated Wolverines were resilient. Brian Griese, whom Price had once recruited, hit Tai Streets for two long touchdowns, sandwiched around Tims's 14-yard touchdown on a reverse, and Michigan led 14–13 entering the fourth period, having blocked the PAT after Tims's score.

"I didn't think they would beat us with the pass," Price says, adding, "we came to play. We were really confident. Part of that's the leadership of Leaf, Chris Jackson, Leon Bender. They were great kids, nice kids, but they were cocky. They were self-confident. They weren't afraid of anything."

But now it was the fourth quarter of the Rose Bowl, and with 11:21 left, Michigan tight end Jerame Tuman wove into the

WSU secondary and caught a 23-yard scoring pass from Griese, making it 21–13. The Cougars got within 21–16 on Lindell's 48-yard field goal midway through the quarter.

Michigan's next drive was excruciating for the Cougars, a 51-yard march. The Wolverines didn't score, but they chipped away valuable seconds with third-down conversions, a couple of them by inches.

Finally, Washington State got the ball back at its own 7 with a mere 29 seconds left. Leaf threw to Taylor for 46 yards and then connected with tight end Love Jefferson, who lateraled to running back Jason Clayton on a truck-and-trailer play to the Michigan 16. Clayton was in the game because Michael Black had sprained an ankle after only seven carries.

With no timeouts left, the Cougars tried to duck in one last snap, but officials ruled that the final two seconds had run out. WSU fans forever cite that lost two seconds, but perhaps it was only justice; it appeared that Taylor may have pushed off Woodson to make his long reception on the final drive.

"As much as I wish we'd have won the game," McWashington says, "I kind of liked the ending, personally. It makes it go down in Rose Bowl lore, like 'What if.'" Besides, despair seemed too extreme for the occasion. Both teams played well; Michigan played slightly better. McWashington's recollection of the postgame scene six weeks before at Husky Stadium is a more fitting description of the bigger picture.

"Who would have thought this?" McWashington said, after the Cougars had cheated history. "Who writes this story?"

Reprise of Roses

Just as many WSU fans couldn't believe it when their team finally made it to the 1997 Rose Bowl for the first time in sixty-seven years, so were they in shock at what happened immediately after that.

The drought was prolonged—true, not sixty-seven years—and painful. From 1998–2000, the Cougars won three Pac-10 games and lost twenty-one. There was a twelve-game losing streak. At least the veneer wasn't indicative of what was underneath. WSU offensive coordinator Mike Levenseller believes the groundwork was laid after the first Rose Bowl, when then-athletic director Rick Dickson signed head coach Mike Price to a contract extension with a mandate: Emphasize high school recruiting, and use the junior colleges only on a "spot" basis. That helped stability.

WSU also had joined the "arms" race in college football, opening a gleaming new weight room and refurbishing offices. And right about the time of the Price extension, the other big

Quarterback Jason Gesser made an unusual transition, going from Honolulu beaches to Palouse wheat fields.

impetus for success was realized. The Cougars, landlocked by wheat fields in eastern Washington, signed a quarterback from, of all places, Honolulu.

Jason Gesser was a different kind of WSU quarterback, a departure from the Jack Thompson–Drew Bledsoe–Ryan Leaf, tall-in-the-saddle triggerman. Gesser was a 6'0" playmaker, a lesser-armed offensive conspirator than those others but one whose smaller stature lent to an inventive, on-the-fly running element. But there was so much more than that. Gesser was a keen student of the game.

"Jason had great vision," said Levenseller. "But he also had such great presence in the pre-snap [reads]." In other words, he got so good at studying film and relating defensive formations to what was about to come at him that, as Levenseller says, "he was really good in knowing where to go with the football." Gesser was also as tough as any WSU quarterback who ever took on the position. He almost seemed to relish the punishment. Bill Drake, the Cougar trainer, got an early taste of that when Gesser, playing at Hawaii late in his redshirt-freshman season of 1999, dove hell-for-leather along the sideline for yardage that seemed meaningless.

"Why'd you do that?" Drake asked.

"I like to take hits," Gesser replied. "Quit trying to tell me not to."

At the same time the Cougars were getting an unwitting assist from their rival across the state. Washington abruptly fired coach Jim Lambright late in 1998, and in the ten-day breach before it hired Rick Neuheisel, the Huskies lost their way in recruiting.

Among those in the state with whom the disconnect cost the Huskies were two future cornerstones of the WSU defense, tackle

Marcus Trufant might have been WSU's best-ever technician at cornerback.

Rien Long and cornerback Marcus Trufant. One would become the 2002 Outland Trophy winner; the other would be taken number eleven in the 2003 NFL draft.

"The Huskies recruited me a little bit," Trufant said. "But as [signing day] came closer they called me and let me know they were pretty much filled up at my position—so, 'Good luck on your college career.'"

Trufant would start as a freshman and by 2002 would become the centerpiece of an outstanding secondary, probably the best in school history. It also included cornerback Jason David and safeties Erik Coleman and Virgil Williams.

If the 1997 team was distinguished mostly by its offense, the 2002 edition won a well-deserved reputation for its defense. Besides the secondary, it featured a sack-happy line—it recorded 52 in the regular season, while WSU allowed 24—bulwarked by Long, plus Jeremey Williams, Fred Shavies, and Isaac Brown. Linebacker Al Genatone was a quiet leader, while New Mexico State transfer Mawuli Davis was undersized but proved a worthy addition.

Gesser was the undisputed leader of the offense. Around him there was a solid line, anchored by first-team all-Pac-10 selections Derrick Roche and Calvin Armstrong. The backfield was shared by Jermaine Green, Jonathan Smith, and John Tippins, and Gesser threw to a corps of tall receivers: Jerome Riley, Mike Bush, and Devard Darling. Another receiver, Collin Henderson, developed a reputation as a "part-time" quarterback. His career as a passer from the wideout spot on trick plays yielded 11 completions in 12 tries for 6 touchdowns and 499 yards.

Nobody had a more unlikely road to Washington State than Darling. He and his twin brother, Devaughn, natives of the Bahamas, had gone to high school in Houston and then joined the program at Florida State. But early in 2001 Devaughn Darling collapsed during a winter workout and died. The brothers carried the genetic trait for sickle-cell anemia, but it could not be determined conclusively whether Devaughn had perished because of the sickling or because of a genetic abnormality. The surviving brother left Florida State and found potential ports of entry

The Cougars went through an exhaustive process before clearing Devard Darling (left) to play.

unwilling to assume the liability of allowing him to transfer in.

Enter the Cougars, who decided to fan out with their team doctors—Dennis Garcia, Ed Tingstad, and Jeff Radakovich—to pick the brains of colleagues in the field to try to make the proper call on Devard. At one point that took Garcia, trainer Drake, and Darling himself to the Seattle office of Dr. Gust Bardy, a University of Washington Medical Center cardiologist, whose work in the case Drake termed "super." He had discussed with a couple of specialists the variables concerning Darling's condition, and the Cougars were persuaded that under the proper supervision of Darling's sickle-cell condition, he could indeed play.

In 2000, with Gesser as a sophomore, the Cougars returned to being competitive. They lost three overtime games, and then they lost Gesser, who sustained a broken leg, but they had regained some saltiness. "That season, 2000, we started to compete again," Levenseller said. "Some people thought of that as being a bad year; I thought it was a hell of a year." Maybe it was, but a lot better ones were on the way.

The year 2001 brought a sharp demarcation in WSU fortunes. The Cougars won ten games—they'd won only ten from 1998 to 2000—and found themselves in an unprecedented position starting 2002. They were picked by Pac-10 media to win the league, the first time in the forty-year history of the poll.

Says Trufant, "I think guys did react like, 'Yeah, we're starting to make our mark now. People are saying there is a team other than the UW in Washington.' A lot of guys used it as fuel for us, to carry a little swagger."

The season was one of strange subplots and oddball sidebars. In the first official game in the newly constructed Seattle Seahawks stadium, WSU used Will Derting's three interceptions—one for a school-record 98 yards and a touchdown—to beat Nevada, 31–7, with 63,588 in attendance. But they allowed 194 second-half rushing yards to freshman Maurice Clarett and an Ohio State team that would win the national championship in a 25–7 WSU defeat, followed by a 49–14 triumph over Idaho.

As it happened, the first real turning point of the season came the following week, against Montana State. In the third quarter of a 45–26 triumph, Gesser took a hard hit in the side from a helmet on a rollout and left the field gasping, hardly able to breathe. He had suffered a dislocated rib. "It's just a tough, tough injury," Drake said. With the Pac-10 schedule dead ahead, it was also an injury that could have sabotaged the season.

First up was Cal, revitalized under first-year coach Jeff Tedford. After the Bears took a 21–6 second-quarter lead, Washington State's season was hanging in the balance. But Gesser, throwing for 431 yards and 4 touchdowns on 28 of 44, played through the pain and led WSU back to a 48–38 victory.

"For some reason, I've always played better when I'm hurt," Gesser said. "I don't know why." No doubt, he is practiced at the art of playing in pain. "I basically had to take shots for seven or eight games in a row," Gesser said. "I was taking painkillers just to practice."

That set up the evening of October 5, 2002, and a game indelibly etched in WSU lore. The seventeenth-ranked Cougars and eighteenth-rated USC played a game worthy of their poll placement—and reflective of the closeness of it. In a contest with five lead changes, WSU had the last one and wedged out a 30–27 victory in overtime, WSU's first success in overtime since the magical 1997 season.

With 1:50 to go, Drew Dunning lined up for a 35-yard field goal as WSU trailed 27–24. For a combination of the momentous and the bizarre, it has to rank as the most unforgettable field goal in WSU history. All it did was leave the Trojans shaking their heads, eventually rerouting them from the Rose to the Orange Bowl. Indirectly, it would also back up Bowl Championship Series selections and delay decisions on almost half the bowl bids. And it would give each Pac-10 school about $400,000, the take from USC's participation in the Orange Bowl. Other than that, it meant nothing.

From the left hash mark, Dunning aimed his attempt over the right guard. But he met the ball too high, and USC defensive tackle Mike Patterson grazed what Dunning called the "inside" of the ball. The belief is that the kick would have hooked wide without the tip. Propelled by crazy English, the ball seemed to swerve abruptly a foot or so inside Dunning's left upright—good, for a 27–all tie. If omens are believable, there could hardly be a noisier one than that.

While Dunning eventually was the hero, the overtime was really testimony to the force of Rien Long. He had two straight tackles for loss on USC's only series before the Trojans missed a field goal. Then Dunning booted one home from 35 yards away and hosted a happy swirl of delirious fans and players at midfield.

WSU followed with routine victories over Stanford, 36–11, and Arizona, 21–13, before the season took a stunning turn the

Drew Dunning had lots of friends after his field goal that upended USC in overtime in 2002.

week the Cougars were to play sixteenth-ranked Arizona State. David and linebacker Ira Davis had a prepractice locker-room fight in which Davis broke David's jaw. "It was a selfish act," said Levenseller. "That act was not indicative of that football team. I'm sure if Ira could have taken it back, he would have. But at that moment, he showed himself to be a selfish person."

Said David, "I went about it as, everything happens for a reason. I kind of took it in stride and bounced back." It could have been a lethal blow, but the Cougars proved to have depth. They inserted sophomore Karl Paymah into David's spot, and the young but gifted Derting moved into the suspended Davis's position. Price decreed that as long as David was out, Davis wouldn't be allowed on the field, either.

"There was a lot of different opinion on how things should be handled, what should go on," Trufant said. "People were angry. I think in the end, the team moved on and came back together as a team."

The ASU game helped take minds off those shenanigans. Gesser threw two touchdown passes in the first six minutes, and the defense didn't allow a Sun Devil touchdown until the fourth quarter of a 44–22 victory on a cold, clear afternoon.

Oregon, the school with the splashy promotional campaigns, was next, providing a contrast to the Cougars' own tongue-in-cheek approach, which was to hang a blow-up poster of Gesser on the side of a grain elevator in tiny Dusty, Washington, 35 miles from Pullman. It was dicey much of the way against the 7–2 Ducks, but WSU pulled away and won 32–21.

The Cougars rose to number three in the polls and at 6–0 in the conference needed only to beat Washington to make it a second Rose Bowl trip in six seasons. Of course, that was easier said than done; the Huskies had won four straight in the series, dating to WSU's Rose-clinching win in Seattle in 1997.

With 9:44 left and WSU clinging to a 17–10 lead, nearly everything—the game, the season, the aspirations—changed. Gesser, scrambling in the backfield to avoid lineman Terry Johnson, had his leg cave in from the pressure of Johnson's weight, suffering a serious "high" ankle sprain.

"That was a difficult thing," said Levenseller. "I think if Jason Gesser stays healthy, he's got control of the football game." Instead, the Huskies came back to tie it at 20 and force overtime, and the teams traded field goals through two extra sessions. Washington's John Anderson put Washington ahead by three in the third overtime, and then came the play that forever will stick in the craw of WSU partisans.

As the Cougars took the ball, backup quarterback Matt Kegel attempted to throw a hitch pass to his left, but it was batted at almost point-blank range by UW defensive end Kai Ellis, who then fell on the ball. Officials conferred, and referee Gordon Riese emerged a moment later with a controversial verdict: It was a lateral, not a forward pass, and therefore Ellis had recovered a fumble. Game over.

Price was livid, and let the officials know it. "I watched so much tape on that afterward," he said. What it showed is something akin to what Pac-10 supervisor of officials Verle Sorgen later conceded: He wouldn't have made the same call. Said Levenseller, "The ball traveled a foot. You don't make that call. You just don't."

The Cougars' big season had taken a terrible turn. Two weeks before a season-ending game at UCLA, it seemed very possible that WSU could fall from a number three ranking all the way to the Holiday Bowl.

Gesser was depressed. Recalling the aftermath, he said, "Those two days were the worst I had as a Washington State Cougar." The unseen hero of that fortnight was Drake, the trainer, who remembers a conversation with Price the day after the Apple Cup. Gesser, hurt and miserable, told Drake and Price, "Well, I'm playing."

"There's no way he'll play, is there?" Price asked Drake as Gesser hobbled off. Drake reserved judgment. He didn't want to give up on Gesser, who certainly wasn't giving up on himself.

"We have a saying in our business," Drake said. "If we're working harder to get better than the patient is, there's a problem. Jason was never in that category."

Behind the scenes there was a funny sequence of events when Drake and Gesser sought to find an orthotic brace that might allow the quarterback to play against UCLA. Eight days after the loss to Washington, they were to take a night flight to Seattle so Gesser could be fitted the next day, but fog enshrouded the Pullman airport 290 miles away. Drake rented the last car available, and they piled into it, Gesser sleeping in the back seat and the two checking into a Seattle motel at 2:00 A.M.

They secured an orthotic, but back in Pullman a couple of days later, Gesser spied another brace in Drake's office, found he liked it better, and the whole venture to Seattle proved to be for naught. "We kept it kind of quiet," Drake said. "The thing cost like $800."

Trainer Bill Drake was an unsung hero in the 2002 season, helping Jason Gesser recover from injuries.

Well before game day, the WSU coaches knew Gesser would start. They didn't know how long he could last, but they'd stick him in the shotgun, try to protect him and hope for the best. Of course, Gesser pooh-poohs any suggestion he wouldn't have played.

"I knew I was gonna play from day one," he said. "But Coach Price said, 'Hey, let's play the role [with the media].' Hey, there was no way I wasn't playing." Gesser's performance was little short of epic, one of the clutch efforts in WSU football history. He played with a football sock over the brace and tape, giving the leg the look of being inflated. He had the mobility of a seventy-five-year-old man, but he threw for 247 yards on 15 of 24 and furthered that reputation of playing through pain. The Cougars won 48–27.

"People talk about being in the zone," Gesser said. "Or finding that clarity. That game got so clear for me. I was picking up every little thing. Everything just seemed so easy."

David returned from his jaw injury and left his signature calling card, an interception. The day was golden for the Cougars. Afterward, they joined a few thousand fans in a corner of the end zone in the WSU fight song and brandished roses for the second time in five years.

Of course, the exuberance would dissolve into controversy ten days later, when Alabama announced Price as its next head coach. For the coaches and those with longtime ties to the program, there was already a sense that 2002 couldn't top 1997. Now this cinched the sentiment, as speculation swirled about whether Price should coach the Cougars in the Rose Bowl or cede the reins to Bill Doba, who was named his successor.

Family Ties

Bill Doba had been at Washington State as a defensive assistant coach for fourteen seasons when he was named to the head position for the 2003 season. And he went looking for the same kind of loyalty and familiarity when he assembled his first staff.

Doba named five WSU alums to his staff. They were Mike Levenseller (1978), Ken Greene (1978), George Yarno (1979), Mike Walker (1982), and Timm Rosenbach (1988). After Doba's third season in 2005, the original staff was still intact.

"I wanted to try to hire people that knew Pullman, had pride in this university, and would stay," Doba said in 2003. "There aren't a lot of Pac-10 schools where you can live, go home for lunch and dinner, and you're five minutes away from the office. And it's a great place to raise a family. I wanted guys who were looking for that."

"The only thing that ruined the year for me was the Alabama decision," Price said. "That just made it kind of messy, which I could never understand, why people didn't want me to coach, to give us the best chance to win. I'd given my blood for 14 years. . . . Gesser would have just freaked out if I wasn't on the sidelines."

Price says even WSU president Lane Rawlins initially opposed his coaching the game but relented when he learned the players favored it.

"I thought he should coach," Doba said. "The guy worked his butt off fourteen years and got us there. To all of a sudden say, 'You can't coach,' it would have screwed up all our game-day preparation." In any case, the thrill was gone. Tickets, scalped for several times face value in 1997, couldn't bring $10 in some cases.

"It was on every player's mind," David said, referring to the coaching transition. "They all talked about it to their friends and their parents, when really they should have been worrying about their game. Even the game didn't feel right."

The Cougars, down 3–0 to Oklahoma near halftime, allowed two touchdowns in the final two minutes and essentially fell out of contention. They had a season-low 243 yards, Gesser was sacked six times, and the Sooners prevailed, 34–14.

Levenseller believes the Rose Bowl hoopla got in the way of Gesser's rehab program. "I don't think we handled that part of it real well," he said. "It's something I learned a lesson from. I don't think I'd allow the media stuff to take place. When you're injured, it's got to take precedence. We were running him around in cars all over the place."

"I don't think he was able to have sharp, crisp practices," Drake concedes. "It was difficult. You're on the road at a bowl trip. We certainly did a lot of treatment, but it was difficult."

The totality of it—Gesser's condition, the turmoil around Price—conspired to leave the Cougars with an emptier feeling than they had known with the Rose Bowl loss to Michigan, when they took their best shot and simply came up short. "I never felt we were into that thing as completely as we were during the season," Levenseller said. "I don't think it was the president's fault for having an opinion, or the A.D.'s fault, but the thing never really got back together. It never got a feel of what it should have been going into that game."

It didn't. Still, Washington State had made it back to Pasadena. And those with an appreciation for history would tell you this: The Cougars did it sixty-two years ahead of schedule.

To Mess with Texas

Jason Gesser remembers the tear-jerking moments in the locker room after Washington State's loss to Oklahoma in the 2003 Rose Bowl. The realization that his career was finished, that a long campaign with his teammates was done. As he addressed the underclassmen, his eyes welled up. "Don't let all the hard work all of us did, getting ten-win seasons in a row, don't let all of this go," Gesser implored. They listened.

The mistake Pac-10 media members made in assessing the 2003 Cougars was in dwelling on what was lost and somehow neglecting to remember what returned. Noting that WSU would be without Gesser, the 2002 offensive coplayer of the year; Rien Long, the Outland Trophy winner; and Marcus Trufant, the number eleven pick in the 2003 NFL draft, the scribes picked the Cougars for seventh in the conference.

It was a bad miscalculation of a team that returned many key parts, including most of its defense. "We had great confidence in ourselves," said safety Erik Coleman, who would go on to start as a rookie with the New York Jets in 2004. "We'd had success, we had a lot of good leaders, and we worked hard."

Those who were firm in the belief that the team would finish seventh were probably just as stunned by the last victory of that season. It came in the Holiday Bowl, against fifth-ranked Texas, and because of the national sway held by the vaunted Longhorns, it ranks among Washington State's most compelling wins in history.

Erik Coleman helped lead the Cougars to three straight ten-win seasons.

"It was just awesome," said Bill Doba, the first-year head coach. "To beat a fifth-ranked team, and in the fashion we did it . . . there was no doubt. For me, that was as fun a win as I've ever had. It goes right up with that Husky win that sent us to the Rose Bowl [in 1997]."

It was the victory that got the Cougars to ten for that season, giving them double digits for the third straight season. Even allowing for the twelve-game regular-season schedules in 2002 and 2003, it was a signal accomplishment, the first time it had been achieved in the Pac-10 since Howard Jones's USC juggernauts of the early 1930s.

They didn't exactly take conventional means to get there. There was WSU's first meeting in history with storied Notre Dame in the second game of the season. The Cougars' veteran defense was a perfect antidote to the offensively challenged Irish, and WSU stormed to a 19–0 second-quarter lead.

But the Cougars wilted in the second half, had to have a miraculous Matt Kegel-to–Sammy Moore touchdown pass in the final minute to send the game to overtime, and lost 29–26. It was a heart-wrenching game they simply should have won. "That game hurt," Coleman admitted, "but at the same time, we got something good out of it."

Indeed, the Cougars didn't mourn long. The Notre Dame game had confirmed to them that they were pretty good, but they needed to complete the project when they got on top rather than sit on it. The next week at Colorado, they exploded to a 47–13 lead and won 47–26.

Then came a routine win at home over New Mexico, followed by a trip to Eugene's Autzen Stadium. It's safe to say that outside of dementia cases, nobody there will ever forget September 27, 2003.

The Ducks were rolling, 4–0 and splashed on the cover of that week's *Sports Illustrated*. They had just upended Big Ten bully

Michigan. It was the perfect setup for WSU, a good team lying in the weeds. "We had a lot of respect for Oregon," said Coleman. "At the same time, we were real tired of hearing about Oregon, about their facilities, how great a program they have. I think they overlooked us." No one could immediately corroborate that autopsy, so buried were the Ducks in their own turnovers.

The Cougars fell on Oregon fumbles. They intercepted passes, a couple of them tipped by linemen who ruined the attempts at the line of scrimmage. They blocked punts. These were the Ducks' twelve first-half possessions, a number bloated by the brevity of most of them: punt, punt, punt blocked, interception, punt, fumble, interception, interception, interception, interception, punt blocked, fumbled kickoff.

A slight underdog, Washington State won, 55–16, setting an opponent record for points scored in Autzen Stadium. The Cougars forced nine turnovers and added the two punt blocks.

Now WSU's "secret" was out. The Cougars won three straight in October before getting handled at eventual national cochampion USC, 43–16. It remained for them to win home games against UCLA and Arizona State before ending the regular season in maddening fashion—again—by losing to Washington in the final moments, 27–19. Coleman can still feel the surface of the football skimming over his fingertips and into the hands of freshman receiver Corey Williams for the winning touchdown.

It was thus a 9–3 regular season, and when the Cougars were paired against Texas in WSU's first Holiday Bowl since 1981, WSU seemed likely to come up one shy of the round numbers of ten victories that year and thirty victories over three years.

The Cougars weren't saying a lot about it, but Kegel's right shoulder, injured in November, still wasn't right. In fact, offensive coordinator Mike Levenseller recalls Kegel trying to throw him a deep ball on the field at Qualcomm Stadium in warm-ups and seeing it die short of the mark. "Rosy [quarterbacks coach Timm Rosenbach] and I tried to keep it a secret," said Levenseller.

Texas was a big 9-point favorite, led by players like running back Cedric Benson, receivers Roy Williams and B. J. Johnson, defensive tackle Marcus Tubbs, and linebacker Derrick Johnson. But the Cougars might have taken heart in a couple of Texas's recent performances as a favorite in San Diego against Northwest teams: In the 2000 Holiday Bowl, Oregon had upset the Longhorns, and a year later Washington took a big lead in the second half before falling victim to a Texas comeback.

"What we saw [on video] going into the game was, they didn't play hard all the time," said Levenseller. "They had tremendous athletes, but they didn't play hard all the time."

The game plan evolved. On offense WSU decided to use lots of four-wide-receiver formations, the better to spread the Longhorn defense. That would allow quick tailback Jonathan Smith to break off some significant gains and keep Texas away from Kegel.

The WSU quarterback was a question mark. Because of that problem shoulder, the Cougars deployed Kegel in the shotgun, something they had avoided most of the season.

Meanwhile, Coleman got a whiff of the defensive plan one day in San Diego, when Ken Greene, the secondary coach, joshed with him before practice. "You could have 15 tackles in this game," Greene said, only half-joking.

The Cougars determined that Texas might be vulnerable to the blitz. The Longhorns liked to "man-protect" or wall off the quarterback from blitzes with simple blocking assignments. Beyond that, Coleman says, "We thought we were able to time up their snap count easily. They'd been doing the same snap count in the shotgun all year. Also, we saw some weaknesses in their line. They weren't as physical as a lot of the teams we had played."

As if their heavy-underdog status didn't afford them enough motivation, the Cougars drew more one day at a luncheon for the teams. Coleman says when a moderator asked one of the Longhorn receivers about the WSU defensive backs, he replied, "They're OK." "It doesn't hurt being underestimated," Coleman said. "We didn't think Texas really respected us too much."

So it was all coming together like a complicated jigsaw puzzle. Except for one thing. The offensive wrinkles the Cougars had tossed into the game plan might as well have been Swahili to the guys running them.

"Man, we just could not get these done," Levenseller said, referring to most of the practices. "The offensive staff was really concerned. The very last practice before the walk-through, it all came together. The offensive staff just looked at each other and went, 'Wow. What just happened?'"

Maybe the defense had something to do with that. Says Greene, "When we got to the practice field, it was not bowl-type practices. They [the defensive players] were getting after it. Our seniors kind of had a chance to put a stamp on their careers and they took it pretty seriously."

Texas had been using two quarterbacks, veteran Chance Mock and freshman Vince Young, so the Cougars were facing some uncertainty. But it was Young who was truly scary, as he would show a year later in the Rose Bowl against Michigan in a record-setting performance.

"We felt we could stack the line, force him to run—and hopefully be able to tackle him," said Greene. "Looking back, the guy that ran the ball [Young] was the most dangerous. That's hindsight."

The teams parried through a scoreless first quarter. But the period ended with Texas on the move, and a couple of minutes into the second quarter, Benson bulled over from the 1 to give the 'Horns a 7–0 lead.

Late in the half, Smith took a screen pass from Kegel and motored 33 yards to the Texas 15, setting up a 12-yard Kegel-to-Moore slant route for a tying touchdown. Momentum swung back to Texas just before the half, however, when running back Selvin Young bolted 48 yards and the 'Horns got a 39-yard field goal four seconds before the break for a 10–7 lead.

But the Cougars owned the third quarter. They turned the game around on their second possession of the half, when Kegel unfurled a perfect bomb to Moore along the right sideline, and he tightroped it in for a 54-yard score, bringing WSU from behind to a 13–10 lead.

It might have looked like clockwork. It was anything but, because of Kegel's ailing shoulder. "Matt came over to the sideline and said he couldn't make that throw," Levenseller said. "We literally had to convince Matt. He said, 'OK.'"

After Texas stalled, Moore burst 51 yards with a Longhorn punt to the Texas 26. It was a pivotal play in a game in which field position was crucial. "That 'flipped' the field," Levenseller said.

Kegel threw to Scott Lunde for a first down at the Texas 12, and then the Cougars went gadget on the Longhorns, unveiling "Smooth Draw," so-called in honor of Smith, their senior back. Kegel trotted right, in motion, and a Longhorn corner went with him. A defensive end turned and ran with the tight end.

Lineman Mike Shelford nullified Tubbs, and Johnson, the All-American linebacker, tripped over a foot in the scrum. After initially dropping the shotgun snap, Smith made a nifty cut and dodged into the end zone. WSU led 20–10.

The Cougars may have won the game on Texas's next possession. Young, who had played most of the game, was pulled for Mock, and the Longhorns faced a fourth-and-three situation at WSU's 39 yard line. It was the kind of play in which Young might have wrought havoc, but Texas stuck with Mock.

Doba was asked eighteen months later if he was all right seeing Mock rather than Young. "Yes, I was," he said, drawing out the words for effect. "I don't know if we could have tackled Vince Young."

On fourth down WSU tackle Tai Tupai penetrated and sacked Mock, who fumbled the ball away to WSU linebacker Will Derting. And in short order WSU's riotous third quarter got even more upbeat; with Texas at its 5, Coleman separated Longhorn Matt Melton from the ball and cornerback Jason David scooped it up and sprinted 18 yards for a touchdown to make it 26–10. "Oh, man, that was exciting," David said. "For my last college game, to score a touchdown was great."

The Longhorns had been backed to their goal line by another uncanny effort from sophomore Kyle Basler, who had a night punters only dream about. He parachuted three boots

Cornerback Jason David's 16 interceptions rank second on the WSU career list.

The Phantom's Long Shadow

Only four decades after he set them are any of Hugh Campbell's (1960–62) school receiving records falling. WSU receiver Jason Hill caught a school-record 13 touchdown passes in 2005, giving him 25 in his career and finally taking down Campbell's forty-three-year-old record of 22. Until Hill overtook Campbell, who was known as the "Phantom of the Palouse," nobody else had come close.

"That's weird, isn't it, with all the passing that school has done," Campbell, president and CEO of the Edmonton Eskimos of the Canadian Football League, told the *Seattle Times*. "It's embarrassing it hadn't been done before. I'm honestly shocked it didn't happen sooner."

Two other Campbell standards are intact: He's at the top of career lists for both receptions (176) and yardage (2,452).

down on the Texas 4 yard line and another at the 5, winning defensive MVP honors.

There were still anxious moments, as a WSU interception late in the game kept Texas in it. The Longhorns scored to get within 28–20 and twice had the ball in WSU territory with a chance to tie it in the last minutes, once at the Cougar 11. But D. D. Acholonu had three sacks in the last three minutes, one resulting in a fumble recovery by Derting, and WSU completed a startling upset.

Smith rambled twenty-one times for 110 yards. The Cougars had seven sacks, and Coleman estimated he personally came on blitzes a shocking fifteen times.

"When I was able to time it, they were never able to see me coming until it was too late," said Coleman. "The games don't get much more fun than that, just running around and making tackles."

If it was a benchmark victory for Washington State, it was also a necessary one. Yes, it was number ten and number thirty, but it was more than that, a triumph over a recognized power on a national stage. In their two recent Rose Bowl marches, the Cougars had pieced together highly memorable seasons—unforgettable seasons—but hadn't been able to finish them with a victory.

This time, they did, and perhaps there was one more legacy left for the future besides the numbers and the magnitude of a resonant bowl victory: Against the odds, they showed what was possible in Pullman.

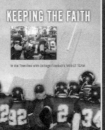
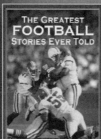